DEVIL'S ADVOCATES

T0341627

DEVIL'S ADVOCATES is a series of books devoted to exploring the classics of horror cinema. Contributors to the series come from the fields of teaching, academia, journalism and fiction, but all have one thing in common: a passion for the horror film and a desire to share it with the widest possible audience.

'The admirable Devil's Advocates series is not only essential – and fun – reading for the serious horror fan but should be set texts on any genre course.'
Dr Ian Hunter, Reader in Film Studies, De Montfort University, Leicester

'Auteur Publishing's new Devil's Advocates critiques on individual titles... offer bracingly fresh perspectives from passionate writers. The series will perfectly complement the BFI archive volumes.' **Christopher Fowler,** *Independent on Sunday*

'Devil's Advocates has proven itself more than capable of producing impassioned, intelligent analyses of genre cinema... quickly becoming the go-to guys for intelligent, easily digestible film criticism.' *Horror Talk.com*

'Auteur Publishing continue the good work of giving serious critical attention to significant horror films.' *Black Static*

 DevilsAdvocatesbooks

 DevilsAdBooks

Also available in this series

The Blair Witch Project Peter Turner

Carrie Neil Mitchell

The Descent James Marriot

Halloween Murray Leeder

Let the Right One In Anne Billson

Saw Benjamin Poole

The Silence of the Lambs Barry Forshaw

The Texas Chain Saw Massacre James Rose

The Thing Jez Conolly

Witchfinder General Ian Cooper

Forthcoming

Antichrist Amy Simmonds

The Curse of Frankenstein Marcus K. Harmes

Dead of Night Jez Conolly & David Owain Bates

Near Dark John Berra

Nosferatu Cristina Massaccesi

Psychomania I.Q. Hunter & Jamie Sherry

DEVIL'S ADVOCATES

BLACK SUNDAY

MARTYN CONTERIO

Acknowledgements

Martyn Conterio would like to thank John Atkinson of Auteur Publishing. Many thanks also to Louise Buckler at Arrow Video, Josh Saco (Cigarette Burns programmer), and the BBFC's Edward Lamberti and Fiona Liddell, who were very helpful in granting me access to the organisation's files on *Black Sunday* and clearing quotations.

For generally being awesome and kind, I'm grateful for knowing these fine folk: Lorraine Conterio, Adriana de Barros, Anton Bitel, Katherine McLaughlin and Neil Mitchell.

This monograph is dedicated to Mario Bava.

First published in 2015 by
Auteur, 24 Hartwell Crescent, Leighton Buzzard LU7 1NP
www.auteur.co.uk
Copyright © Auteur 2015

Series design: Nikki Hamlett at Cassels Design
Set by Cassels Design www.casselsdesign.co.uk
Printed and bound by CPI Group (UK) Ltd, Croydon, CR0 4YY

British Library Cataloguing-in-Publication Data
A catalogue record for this book is available from the British Library

ISBN: 978-1-906733-83-4
ebook ISBN: 978-1-906733-89-6

CONTENTS

INTRODUCTION

Mario Bava made his officially credited directorial debut with *La maschera del demonio* (*The Demon's Mask*). The film took inspiration from a 19th century short story, *Viy*, written by Ukrainian author Nikolai Gogol. In the United States, American International Pictures released the picture as *Black Sunday*. The film starred Barbara Steele, John Richardson, Arturo Dominici, Andrea Checchi and Ivo Garrani.

A WORD ON THE FILM'S TITLE

The Italian-language title, *La maschera del demonio*, can be read as a pun, a homage to, or rip-off of Hammer's 1957 production *The Curse of Frankenstein*, exhibited in Italy as *La maschera di Frankenstein*. The Warner Bros. 3D horror marvel, *The House of Wax* (1953), also bore 'La maschera' in the title when released as *La maschera di cera* (*The Wax Mask*).

American International Pictures (AIP) purchased North American distribution rights and re-edited scenes, redubbed the soundtrack and dialogue, changed character names and gave it an entirely new identity: *Black Sunday*. In England, during 1968, it received a theatrical run as *Revenge of the Vampire*. (There are other alternative titles floating around including *House of Fright*.)

Whatever one's overall judgement of the AIP cut, *Black Sunday*, as a title, fits the Gothic and plangent mood much better than *The Mask of Satan* or the utterly naff *Revenge of the Vampire*. I would even argue it is better than *La maschera del demonio*. 'Black', in this context, too, resonated with the saturnine but elegant countenance of Barbara Steele's role as Katia, as well as a suitably apt description of evil – and *dead* sexy – ancestor Asa (also played by Steele). AIP's alteration also aligned the film closer to Gogol's tale, by virtue of the creation of a faux folkloric tradition that gave context to the overall plot action. Fixing narrative events around a historical date bestowed upon the movie a wonderful portent of doom: '*One day in each century, it is said that Satan walks the earth. To the God-fearing, this day is known as Black Sunday*.' The clever alteration to *The Mask of Satan*'s soundtrack (Tim Lucas suggests either dubbing producer Lou Rousoff or director Lee Kresel made the change) produced a satanic frisson: a reversal of Christ's resurrection from beyond the grave on Easter Sunday. We witness the Passion of Asa and her return two hundreds year later on … Black Sunday.

If the Italian-language title attached itself to André de Toth's *House of Wax* or Hammer's *Frankenstein* picture then it has been suggested AIP were reminded of *Black Friday* (1940), a B-picture starring Boris Karloff, Bela Lugosi and co-written by Curt Siodmak. AIP also considered other titles, such as *Witchcraft*, *The Curse* and *Vengeance*.

But, let's face it, putting the word 'black' into any horror film title just sounds damn cool and invokes the appropriate – and required – amounts of audience expectation, fear and menace. Bob Clark flipped *White Christmas* (1954) into *Black Christmas* (1974). Unless you're a complete bloody sadist and/or rank sentimentalist, you'd watch Clark's proto slasher every time.

In 1992, just over thirty years on from the release of *Black Sunday*, the film's rights reverted back to Italian producers and an English dubbed version (initially prepared for AIP) was licensed to Redemption Video. This version was passed by the BBFC on 10th November 1992 and awarded the '15' certificate. *The Mask of Satan* was released on VHS and has threatened, with its explicit violence and other uncensored moments, to overshadow the AIP version ever since. So much so that the English-language 'Director's Cut' could not be ignored in the writing of this monograph. But wait there a minute!

Why the preference for *Black Sunday* over this alternative English-language version that is now widely seen thanks to VHS, DVD and Blu-ray and which is essentially Bava's cut replaced with an English dubbed soundtrack and dialogue? Simply because the AIP version was – like a lot of folk – how I first became introduced to the film and the world of Mario Bava. The AIP cut might stick one in the eye to *auteur* theory, but it is the version which spread his name and reputation abroad. So yes, AIP might have changed more than a few things (with mixed results – see chapter 3), but its cinematic power and the imagination and genius of Bava is undiminished.

The monograph shall refer to the film throughout as *Black Sunday* with reference, where applicable, to *La maschera del demonio* and *The Mask of Satan*.

Synopsis

The year is 1630. In the principality of Moldavia, Princess Asa of the House of Vajda, and her accomplice Javuto, have each been condemned to die as vampires and for consorting with Satan.

Asa, in her very last moments, curses the bloodline of the Grand Inquisitor (and her older brother) Griabe, warning that one day she will return from beyond the grave to exact revenge. Griabe commands the executioner to hammer the Mask of Satan on to Asa's face. He then gives the go-ahead for the stake to be lit. A thunderstorm suddenly rages and Asa's body is unable to be burned. The crowd scatters.

Two hundred years later, Dr. Thomas Kruvajan and his colleague Dr. Andreas Gorobec are passing through Moldavia on their way to a medical conference. Kruvajan orders the driver to take a short cut through the forest road and to stop for the night at the village of Mirgorod. A wheel of the carriage comes off on the old and unpaved lane. Waiting for their superstitious driver to fix it, they wander to a nearby set of chapel ruins – attracted by a whistling noise – and inspect the crypt, where Kruvajan relates the story of the cursed Vajdas. They discover the well-preserved corpse of Asa lying in her tomb. Kruvajan unwisely removes the Mask of Satan. A giant bat attacks the older man, which he shoots with a revolver and beats with his cane. Gorobec notices the older doctor has cut his hand. Droplets of blood drip onto the waxen skin and into the eye sockets of Asa.

Walking back through the ruins, the carriage now fixed and waiting, Kruvajan and Gorobec meet Princess Katia and her two large hounds. She is the exact image of her wicked ancestor killed two centuries ago. Gorobec appears instantly smitten with the princess.

Meanwhile, Kruvajan's blood has acted as a reviving agent to Asa's corpse and she calls out to Javuto, who stirs from his slumber in a nearby graveyard to set about their diabolical plan/promise made two hundred years ago. Javuto goes to the castle and terrifies Prince Vajda. The troubled prince attempts to ward the vampire off with a crucifix before succumbing to a state of catatonia.

Kruvajan, resting in Mirgorod village inn, is called to the castle by Katia and her brother Constantin, but the messenger, Boris, is intercepted and murdered by Javuto. Kruvajan is taken to see Asa instead, who has not yet been restored to full power. She turns the poor doctor into a vampire's consort. Asa's plot is to drain the lifeforce of Katia and walk free again upon the earth. Kruvajan, now one of the undead, is sent to the castle to turn Prince Vajda into a bloodsucking fiend.

The innkeeper's daughter, who witnessed Asa's demon helper take away Kruvajan, informs Gorobec of what she saw. A priest recognises, too, that Javuto has returned from the grave and must be stopped. The priest and Gorobec search the local graveyard and discover the sleeping body of Kruvajan. The priest thrusts a stake into the man's eye, killing him.

At the castle, Javuto has located Katia and taken her by force to meet Asa. Gorobec enters the crypt and finds Asa pretending to be Katia. The real Katia is sleeping on the coffin. She informs the love-struck hero to stake the vampire whilst he still has the chance! Asa gives herself away because Katia is wearing a small silver crucifix around the neck, something the witch would find intolerable, given her allegiance to Satan. Asa's ruse is called out. She opens her robe to reveal a skeletal form. In the nick of time, the priest and villagers turn up to save the day and Asa is tied to a stake (again) and set alight. She is killed (again). Like Sleeping Beauty, Katia awakes.

1. CONTEXT

THE EARLY YEARS

Mario Bava was born on 29th July 1914 in Sanremo, Liguria, a province that sits in the far north-east corner of Italy, nestled beneath Piedmont and playing next-door neighbour to the French Riviera. As a '*figlio d'arte*' (child of the arts) his ties to the film world were provided his father, the sculptor and cinematographer Eugenio Bava (1886 – 1966), whose artistry and pioneering experimental photography was utilised in the burgeoning Italian movie-making industry of the 1900s.

Young Bava started his own journey into the business in the 1930s. He began at LUCE (L' Unione Cinematografica Educativa, founded 1924) in the optical effects department. According to Tim Lucas' extensive research and the subsequently published filmography, found in the pages of *Mario Bava: All The Colors of the Dark* (2007), he earned his stripes in various departmental subdivisions: main title design, animation and special trick photography. During these formative years – and into the 1940s and 1950s – he was hired (in various capacities) on projects that today serve to highlight the director's remarkable place in post-war Italian cinema. Like Woody Allen's chameleon character Leonard Zelig, Bava seemed to be there at decisive industry moments and played a part in the launching of genres whose best pictures are today praised and loved as cult classics. There's even an association with Neo-realism. Bava can take no responsibility or credit for popularising the Spaghetti Western, but he did eventually make one (*The Road to Fort Alamo*, 1964). The same goes for hugely successful 'sex comedies'.

One of the most interesting aspect of the director's personality, given his chosen field of work (low-budget genre pictures often involving themes of horror), was how many colleagues, friends and family members attested to Bava having been genuinely afraid of the dark. Ghost stories and the fantastical stuff of nightmares disturbed him on a profound level. This shouldn't be so surprising. By all accounts, he was a sensitive and very modest man. '*My dreams are always horrible,*' Bava once stated, '*there's a character that continuously haunts me in my nightmares, he's a musician that serenades his lover with a violin, strings with the nerves of his own arm*'. (Pirie, 1977: 158)

During the first interview with him ever to appear in print, for the magazine *Horror*, and under the article headline '*The Hitchcock of Cinecittà*', Bava further elucidated, though still managing to be evasive at the same time, on his attraction to morbid themes:

> Terror fascinates and attracts me, but for no particular reason. Perhaps it's a question of psychology … to make a film of this kind helps me overcome my own fears. The lights, the technicians, and the actors help to defuse an atmosphere that, in real life, would be enough to make me die of fright. (Lucas, 2007: 18)

BEFORE BLACK SUNDAY

In 1956 a low-budget film was produced titled *I vampiri* (*The Vampires*). Bava stepped in not only to complete the picture, but reconceptualised it after the director, Riccardo Freda, walked off set (see chapter 2). *I vampiri* was actually Italy's first proper foray into Gothic territory since 1921. Bava's career as a credited film-maker, however, did not proceed in earnest from this landmark production. He returned to work as a renowned cameraman and hired hand on a number of pictures that included *Hercules* (*Le fatiche di Ercole*, 1958) starring Steve Reeves, a film that kick-started a popular cycle of Pepla (Sword-and-Sandal flicks).

Further evidence of Bava's propensity to be in the right place at the right time, after *I vampiri* and *Hercules*, he became involved with the European co-production, *Death Came from Outer Space* (US title: *The Day The Sky Exploded*, 1958). Tim Lucas has written that Italy's first-ever sci-fi flick was Bava's debut as a director in all but name. Owing to several factors – such as the financial backers requiring somebody with proper experience at calling the shots – he received no official acknowledgment. Paolo Heusch, a name forgotten today, bagged the 'directed by' credit.

In 1959, Bava teamed up once more with Riccardo Freda to make *Caltiki – Il Mostro Immortale* (*Caltiki – The Immortal Monster*). Again, he was left to complete the movie after Freda walked off set. After employment on Jacques Torneur's *The Giant Marathon* (1959), producers recognised beyond doubt that this shy and retiring cameraman/effects magician/problem-solver could be a great director whose invention and panache was impressive, even if the material could be sub-par. Most importantly (for the producers, at least), he finished on time and kept within the confines of the budget. Bava's career in the Italian film industry, before making his debut proper, explained why *Black Sunday* made such an instant impact.

THE AUTEUR SITUATION OF SIGNOR HORROR

Although we look to critics and reviewers to guide our taste and define the cinematic milieu in popular culture, we cannot always rely on them to get things right first time round. Some film-makers are not immediately recognised and it can take years for retrospective opinion to take hold. The word 'genius' crops up time and time again, where Mario Bava is concerned. But how can a man who spent twenty years directing schlocky fare and *filoni* ('formula films', but also a complicated term with subtle distinctions within industry and critical study) ever be considered for membership to the pantheon of the medium's greatest talent? Aren't these coveted spaces reserved for the lofty likes of D.W. Griffith, Jean Renoir, Sergei Eisenstein and other prestigious types? What Andrew Sarris referred to as a '*Ptolemaic constellation of directors in a fixed orbit,*' and something he actually cautioned against (1962: 563).

His first picture was feted by critics, but there seemed to be a subsequent disappointment. Many things worked against the director, such as his lack of control with foreign distributors re-cutting his work willy-nilly. Snobbery against the horror genre shouldn't be discounted, either. His reputation dwindled somewhat with reviewers and writers lamenting that he never fulfilled the promise of his debut. A more recent assessment, based on a revival of interest, has helped re-establish the director as one of the medium's true masters and many today consider him worthy of *auteur* status even if such a term doesn't carry the weight it once did.

In the 1990s, several major retrospectives were held in France (the country that took note of Bava very early on), the UK and USA. Directors such as Martin Scorsese and Tim Burton began to discuss what Bava meant to them and paid homage, via visual or narrative quotations, in their own work. Joe Dante went one further and cast Barbara Steele in *Piranha* (1977). Scorsese purloined from *Kill, Baby … Kill!* (1966) the concept of an evil spirit in the guise of a small child for his controversial *The Last Temptation of Christ* (1988).

In Julian Petley's review of *City of the Living Dead* (*Film & Filming*, June 1982), the critic highlighted a comment made by Lucio Fulci, who became known as the 'Godfather of Gore' after a raft of surrealistic pictures in the late 1970s and into the 1980s, that acknowledged Bava's cultural standing and its eventual shift. '*Bava's films, too, rest on their technical aspect, their special effects and suspense: they've thus really no need of actors. But Bava was despised in Italy: he and Freda were ignored and critics spoke of the genius of Bava only after his death*' (1982: 33).

Scorsese provided the introduction to Tim Lucas' *Mario Bava: All The Colors of the Dark* (2007):

> Bava was not a great storyteller, but he didn't have to be and he wasn't trying to be. He was good – very good – at something else. He used light, shadow and color, sound (on and off-screen), movement and texture down uncharted paths into a kind of collective dream. (2007: 13)

Interviewed for an Italian television documentary, *Operazione Paura* (2004), Hollywood kook Tim Burton also noted this dream ambience: '*They were so much truly like bringing dreams to life.*' Roger Corman, interviewed for the same documentary, and a man who knows a thing or two about financial prudence and working on miniscule budgets, reasoned that not only were the films themselves so remarkable, the man's sense of professionalism was equally admirable: '*His genius – and I really do believe it was a genius – and an inspiration to those who came after him, was that whatever the circumstance or situation, you can do excellent work.*'

We live in age where *auteur* theory is less celebrated as a model of critical study than it was in its heyday. In whatever guise or model, it has remained popular – the director is still the focus of obsession – and it has been appropriated today as a marketing tool. The term 'vulgar auteurism' has been banded around, too, as a way to highlight genre film-makers whose work previously has been unappreciated by mainstream critics. In many ways, auteur theory is tailor-made for Bava. Whether you dig the auteurist approach as a critical avenue of exploration or loathe it as romantic nonsense, it's a war that we must brave. Take a side, if you will.

Could Mario Bava qualify as an *auteur* film-maker? The question has been asked many times over the years, and with a range of affirmatives and dismissals. Using the Sarris theory, while it has remained absolutely clear that Bava's work was routinely compromised and changed, he did boast a distinct visual authority and stamp and was more than technically competent (the use of the crash zoom, Joe Dante has jokingly claimed, approached abuse of technique) and the dysfunctional family unit is a theme/ scenario that has cropped up. It must be noted, too, that he was very often the cinematographer and camera operator on his own pictures (sometimes credited and sometimes not). He was very hands-on in the special effects departments (again, taking no credit) and worked on stories and scenarios. His modesty forbade credit-hogging.

One magazine declared him 'Signor Horror'. Journeymen film-makers do not earn nicknames, it must be said. In terms of film culture, being labelled an *auteur* (and being named 'Signor Horror') are also marketable assets. We often describe thrillers as 'Hitchcockian'. In a fair world – if he was a household name and not a cult figure – 'Bavian' would be an equally popular term. Looking at the career of Mario Bava, in total, he is an exceptional case and clearly an influential film-maker – not only on genres but other directors. He was no mere journeyman, for sure.

Julian Petley likened Bava to his compatriot, Lucio Fulci, in the *City of the Living Dead* review for *Film & Filming* and qualified both as *metteur en scène* directors. (I've always thought this the critically polite way of saying 'close but no cigar'.) But can a *metteur en scène* become an *auteur*? Although Pauline Kael accused the Sarrisian model of potentially elevating what could be deemed trivial matters to the heights of high art and focusing on a director's filmography as a series of dull repetitions, it can prove useful enough, however limited one ultimately deemed it. Whether you think Bava a supreme visual stylist alone or an out-and-out *auteur*, it's a matter of staking an opinion.

IT'S REVIVED!

1960 is considered a fine vintage year in the illustrious and often controversial annals of horror cinema. Not only did Mario Bava, at the relatively late age of 45, make his credited directorial debut, Georges Franju's *Eyes Without a Face*, Michael Powell's *Peeping*

Tom, Roger Corman's *The Fall of the House of Usher*, and of course, Alfred Hitchcock's *Psycho*, all presented latent fears in public spaces. Roger Vadim, too, helped establish the lesbian vampire subgenre with *Blood and Roses*, a reworking of Sheridan Le Fanu's *Carmilla* (1872). Whether it was human monsters (what Charles Derry described as an entirely new subgenre, 'the horror of personality') or old fashioned supernatural beasts at the centre of the narrative storm, the genre entered new territory, where directors pushed the envelope, the censors frowned and most critics bothered. Directors pushed the envelope and audiences lapped it up. These flicks brought peculiar, sick, strange and unseemly relationships to the fore and taboo subject matters appeared in clearer focus. Writer and historian Carlos Clarens (1930–1987) stated the horror movie was something of a historical imperative and worked as a mass psychotherapy session. I very much admire, too, the simple but searching question posed by Charles Derry: '*Why is the world so horrible?*' (1977: 82).

Kim Newman in *Nightmare Movies* stated: '*To me, the central thesis of horror in film and literature is that the world is a more frightening place than is generally assumed*' (1988: 5). H.P. Lovecraft, Bava's favourite author, noted in his essay, 'Supernatural Horror in Literature': '*The oldest and strongest emotion of mankind is fear, and the oldest and strongest kind of fear is fear of the unknown*' (Lovecraft, 1927: 7).

In the English-speaking world, writers such as Clarens, Ivan Butler and Robin Wood began to twig that the genre was indeed something that would benefit from being prized apart from alignments to fantasy pictures and could stand alone and be worthy of serious critical exploration. Firstly, why did audiences pay hard-earned money to essentially be frightened out of their wits? According to Clarens there is '*Inside us a constant, ever-present yearning for the fantastic, for the darkly mysterious, for the choked terror of the dark*' (Clarens, 1968: 9), and Derry argued for our '*subconscious need to deal with things that frighten us*' (1977: 21).

Perversion, psychological torments and madness, irrationality, eroticism, brutal death and the supernatural all mingled freely. The Marquis de Sade wrote once that '*There is no better way to know death than to link it with some licentious image*' (Bataille, 1957: 11). This statement rings loudest and truest in the vampire genre, where the link between sex and death is absolutely vital and can play host to a range of visual metaphors and symbols. We can ban, censor and repress as much as we like, but kink will out.

Black Sunday is a film that takes place within a sub-category Charles Derry defined as the 'horror of the demonic'. Here, supernatural forces can explain away the evil of our world and that moral/social order can be maintained via the eternal battle between Good and Evil. The essence of *Black Sunday* – and the general theme of 'horror of the demonic' – is centred on corruption of the innocence and an open attack on the everyday order of things. One is natural and the other unnatural and must be fought against and destroyed before equilibrium can be restored.

Films such as *Black Sunday* helped the horror genre gain a certain cache as titles worthy of study. In Theodore Roszak's novel, *Flicker* (1991), two characters exchange views that cleverly highlighted the often luckless artistic and critical value of horror films. A rather haughty German director, a guest at a stereotypically libertine Hollywood producer's house party, tells a fleapit theatre owner and sometime critic: '*Surely you aren't suggesting we give trash like Feast of the Undead serious critical attention!*' (1991: 99).

Although dealing with titles at the grindhouse end of the genre spectrum (and erroneously suggesting there was nothing much happening in the UK or American cinema) authors Cathal Tohill and Peter Tombs (in *Immoral Tales: Sex and Horror Cinema in Europe 1956 – 1984*) pointed out, quite rightly, that the flood gates had been opened to new cinematic possibilities at this key time.

During the 1960s and 1970s, the European horror film went totally crazy. It began to go kinky, creating a new type of cinema that blended eroticism and horror. This heady fusion was highly successful, causing a tidal wave of celluloid weirdness that was destined to look even more shocking and irrational when it hits countries like England the USA (1994: 155).

This is not to draw a line in the sand and suggest that anything before was half-formed, incomplete or that the genre (and its various subgenres and cross pollinations) spent years in some sort of unimaginative wasteland before discovering its true purpose and growing up proper. Movies do not exist in a vacuum nor do they arrive by Immaculate Conception! It could be argued, too, that film-makers under strict studio/producer guidelines and various codes of screen conduct had more of a challenge, and therefore fun, inserting or insinuating transgressive themes or weird beats into hack jobs than having carte blanche as film creatives do today. If it was true that the genre (though not as easily defined as a distinct 'type' we would often like) was some backwater creek before 1960, how to explain something like *Freaks* (1932). A film produced by MGM, the grandest and richest studio of old Hollywood.

The big screen has always illuminated the dark realities of our world. James Whale's *The Old Dark House* (1932) dared to probe generational conflict and insanity. He masked it as an eccentric farce. The character Horace Femm (played wonderfully by Ernest Thesiger) and his irrational fear of fetching a lamp from the house's upper landing is a striking piece of psychological terror that foreshadows all sorts of modern horror avenues. Carl Theodor Dreyer's *Vampyr* (1932), perhaps too avant garde for popular taste and a flop on release, is a startlingly zonked-out motion picture discussed today quite rightly as a masterpiece. In the 1940s, producer Val Lewton's films with director Jacques Tourneur ingeniously presented the haunted mind with trick photography and shadows. Another incredibly mad film produced during the initial American craze for horror films was Erle Kenton's *Island of Lost Souls* (1932). A literary adaptation of a prestigious author's work, it demonstrated a fine capacity to disturb both studio executives and the audience. Forget all about entertainment and art for a second – it made viewers feel something other than a traditional fright. There is something not quite right about *Freaks* and *Island of Lost Souls*, despite their forward-thinking tolerance to errors of the human body and sexual frankness: whether that's a wealthy circus midget marrying a capricious Russian beauty or a hero getting the horn for a sexy panther lady (played by the comely Kathleen Burke), in the latter. If only Dr. Moreau (Charles Laughton) had been attentive enough to have manicured Lota's furry panther hands!

A CERTAIN SENSE OF DECLINE

Genres and their popularity move in cycles. For one to revise its rules and appeal there must be a certain sense of decline to have occurred or – at the very least – a lull. Into the late 1940s and 1950s, a few years after two atomic bombs (Fat Man and Little Boy) were dropped on Japanese cities, though horror movies were still being made, sci-fi flicks (with aliens from outer space threatening our earthly extinction) became king.

Creature Features and political paranoia collided. Movies with Gothic figures were being produced, for sure, but they bore titles such as *Mother Riley Meets the Vampire* (1952) and *I was a Teenage Frankenstein* (1957). In works such as *The Thing from Another World* (1953), *The Quatermass Xperiment* (1955) or the 1954 novel by Richard Matheson, *I Am Legend*, the vampire-like traits of the monsters presented apocalyptic jeopardy, far from the Gothic incarnation made popular in the 1920s and 1930s. However, sex and death and violence would return in a more virulent and brazenly explicit fashion thanks to Hammer Films and others.

2. THE BIRTH OF ITALIAN HORROR

THE POST-WAR ITALIAN FILM INDUSTRY

The rise of Italian genre cinema and its venerable golden age was assisted by financial incentives and funding awards. It was not simply a concerted effort to counter Hollywood's cultural dominance and favour homemade product. Producers and other executives wished to expand their horizons. Lucrative contracts and opportunities do not require borders, after all, and there would be clear and welcome advantages to international co-productions and distribution deals. Rome did not earn the moniker 'Hollywood on the Tiber' for nothing. Foreign dough – American, French, German and Spanish – was most vital to Italy's flourishing success during this period. American producers began buying up low-budget genre pictures to flog at home. Turning a profit wasn't difficult. *Black Sunday* became a stellar success in the United States when released in 1961. '*From 1957 to 1967 US companies spent approximately $35 million dollars a year to finance or buy the distribution rights to Italian films, or to make their own films, with Italian studios as their production base*' (Baschiera & Di Chiara, 2010: 11).

Galatea, the production outfit that financially backed Bava's film, branched out to the American market when they sold *Hercules* to producer Joe Levine and subsequently earned an advance to provide a sequel. '*From then on, even smaller producers knew that there existed American distributors who were willing to pay an advance for genre movies, and even for genres that Italian audiences did not like*' (ibid: 33).

In 1956, the chief executive officer of Titanus, Goffredo Lombardo, announced the crisis facing Italian cinema was due to a heavy dependence on making pictures for the home audience. He came up with an idea to bolster production as well as profits:

> While lowbrow pictures were to be made just for Italian spectators with Italian funds, medium-sized productions should instead be made with European investors and should be aimed at the European market; eventually, Italian cinema should also attempt large productions in partnership with American studios, with the goal of reaching a global market (ibid: 32).

The boost in feature production during the 1950s was partly due to the inviting cultural/ economic protection model by Christian Democrat politician, Guilo Andrelotti. A loan fund was set up which was '*fed by taxes on foreign film dubbing, an automatic tax refunds system (about ten percent of the film's gross) and a special norm (introduced in 1951) which forbade the export of 50 per cent of the gross made in Italy by every foreign film, thus forcing Hollywood to invest part of their income in Italian productions*' (ibid.).

ITALIAN HORROR

A major accusation that has followed Italian genre movies around for decades, like the fetid stink of a zombie from one of Fulci's grotty horror picture shows, is that it merely existed, even thrived like a parasite, on an endlessly crass appropriation and replication of popular – and especially Hollywood – genres. Nowhere was this accusation more alive than with the Spaghetti Western. In his seminal study of the genre, *Spaghetti Westerns: Cowboys and Europeans from Karl May to Sergio Leone* (1981), Sir Christopher Frayling explained the whole system's inner workings:

> Between the early 1950s and mid-1960s, Italians (and later Spanish) producers working at Cinecitta Studios had made various attempts to anticipate (or exploit) the taste of the Italian urban cinemagoers, by hijacking entire film genres – the most notable being the 'filmfumetto' (1948–1954), the farcical comedy, often of a dialect kind (1955–1958), the 'sword and sandal' epic (1958–1964), the horror film (1959–1963), the World By Night or Mondo Cane genre (1962–1964), and the spy story derived from James Bond (1964–1967). Many of these Cinecittà films were made in assembly-line circumstances which resembled those of Hollywood B features, or even TV series: shooting schedules which seldom over-ran a five-six week was normal; budget averaging $200,000; the more solid sets used over and over again; only two or three takes per shot; post-synchronised sound and dialogue tracks (even in Italian versions). (1981: 68)

Italians loved movies during this fallow period. But they loved certain kinds of movies. From Milan to Naples to Brindisi way down in the boot heel south, patrons went to the pictures as a recreational pastime more than any other European nation during the post-war years.

A major reason, perhaps *the* major reason, for Italy's failure to establish its own variation on the horror movie was on political grounds. Mussolini's reign as dictator saw the industry stifled by fascist meddling. The government banned American films outright in 1938. Yet in an exceedingly perverse way the fascists established, in these years, the Istituto Nazionale LUCE, the Centro Sperimentale di Cinematografia and built world-class facilities – Cinecittà – as well as set up 'cinema caravans' that toured rural and remote regions of the country. The sound era also saw the establishment of post-dubbing the soundtracks, by which the authorities could easily control the information imparted; mostly importantly, the dialogue. British director Peter Strickland made an entire film centred on this industry peculiarity in 2012's *Berberian Sound Studio*.

One would expect a country such as Italy, the land that posited the bloody spectacle of Christians being thrown to lions and/or gladiators in the coliseums of its vast empire counted as a thoroughly entertaining afternoon out, that gave us bloody Renaissance paintings and the eternal degradation and phantasmal terror in the *Inferno* and *Purgatory* of Dante Alighieri's *The Divine Comedy* (written between 1308–1321), to have been a prime candidate to pioneer horror cinema all on their own. Violence is Italian art, as Lucio Fulci quipped.

THE MONSTER OF FRANKENSTEIN

Prior to the Italian Gothic boom, which lasted from roughly 1960 to 1965, only the lost silent *Frankenstein* adaptation sticks out from the crowd. In 1921 Eugenio Testa directed – a whole year before F.W. Murnau delivered his unofficial Dracula (*Noserfatu: A Symphony of Horror*) – *Il Mostro di Frankenstein* (*The Monster of Frankenstein*) from a script by Giovanni Drovetti. This, however, was not the first *Frankenstein* adaptation to grace the silver screen. There were two silent features produced in 1910 and 1915, one an Edison production and then *Life without a Soul*, directed by Joseph W. Smiley, respectively. Both of these are American productions. *Il Mostro di Frankenstein* was a German-backed effort made in Italy by Testa (1892–1957), an actor and director.

Needless to say, it doesn't get any more Gothic than Mary Shelley's acclaimed novel inspired by a nightmare experienced during her stay at the Villa Diodati in June 1816 –

an infamous summer that has entered into literary lore. *Il Mostro di Frankenstein* starred Linda Albertini, Luciano Albertini (credited as Baron Frankenstein), and Umberto Guarracino took the role of 'The Monster'. Guarracino was a strongman type in several Peplums.

The film posed serious problems for the Italian censors and forced the makers to cut the picture so drastically that the release length was a mere thirty-nine minutes. *Il Mostro di Frankenstein* was reduced to the status of a featurette.

As a further point to the sensitivities stoked in general by screen adaptations of *Frankenstein*, James Whale's version (1931)suffered at the hands of the censors a decade later when the newly established 'Production Code' was in force. The re-release of *Frankenstein*, prior to *The Bride of Frankenstein* (1935), excised the line: '*Now I know what it feels like to be God!*'

The intensity and amount of scene removal from Testa's film by the censors suggested the material was simply deemed too strong for the audience to stomach. The Catholic sensibility could not take such an affront to their teachings and way of life by some entertainment venture. As with a vast majority of movies produced during the early years, *Il Mostro di Frankenstein* is today considered a lost film. A production still is extant along with a couple of posters. One piece of promotional material advertised a screening at the Selection Georges Petit, 37, Rue de Trovise, Paris. The other announced the film, advertised in 1926 (so still around five years after release), playing with a Hal Roach directed two-reeler starring Harold Lloyd. What on earth to make of that double bill? After that, *Il Mostro* vanished into the murky abyss of history. It is worth noting that at the bottom of the 1926 promotional poster there is an advertisement for a peplum titled *Galaor contra Galaor*, made in 1924, and a film attributed to Eugenio Bava.

A MAJOR STEP FORWARD: I VAMPIRI

The theatrical release of *I vampiri* (known internationally as *The Devil's Commandment* and *Lust of the Vampire*) on 5th April 1957 gave subsequent Italian Gothic a foundation on which to build its place in history. Shot in the autumn of 1956 it preempted Hammer's foray into Gothic by a year even though the story is not set in the 19th century and neither is it exclusively Gothic in tone. Yet Freda and Bava might as well have declared on the studio floor at Titanus, St. Peter-like, 'Upon this film, we shall build Italianate horror'. '*With* I vampiri/The Devil's Commandment *the Italian gothic horror film emerged fully formed and apparently out of nowhere*' (Hughes, 2011: 155).

I vampiri is inarguably the bedrock, the grandfather, the instigator of Italian horror cinema. It was never heralded as such until many years later, and flopped when sent out to the picture houses of Italy. Neither is there much in the way of gore, eroticism or romance. Compare it to Hammer Films' output a year or so later and *I vampiri* is positively chaste. It has been written Freda's original concept would have been more gruesome than the finished product, which was revised extensively by Bava, who worked at the behest of his paymasters, as well as basically saving the entire film from disaster. The major stumbling block for any more films in the immediate aftermath of *I vampiri's* Italian release – that worked against any prospective foray into the genre – was the salient fact that movies of this type that derived from the studios of Rome were not taken at all seriously by filmgoers, who thought the whole notion of 'Italian horror' quite off-putting. It was a cultural thing; a matter of indifference and sense of cultural inferiority. Freda, in a reminiscence included in the Arrow Video Blu-ray release booklet of *Black Sunday*, recalled:

> The first horror film I did was *I vampiri* in 1957. The film did not go down too well, it was perhaps a little ahead of its time for audience tastes, but above all the people who followed that genre of cinema only did so if the film was American. I was there at San Remo for the premiere. As people filled into the cinema, they stopped to look at the photographs and the names. When they arrived at mine, they exclaimed: 'My God, it's an Italian film then!' Then they left. (2013: 28)

When it came to making *Caltiki – the Immortal Monster*, in 1959, Freda decided upon a cunning ruse. He would change the names of actors and the production crew in order to fool the audience into thinking they were watching a foreign movie.

HOW I VAMPIRI CAME INTO BEING

Riccardo Freda (1909–1999), an Egyptian-born Italian national, had been involved in the film industry since 1937. The story goes that he made a bet with two producers that he could shoot a picture in twelve days. Freda had met Bava on the set of *Spartaco* in 1953 (US title: *Sins of Rome*). They clicked over a mutual passion for the arts. One day, Mario invited his new buddy Riccardo back home to look at Eugenio's wax sculptures and they hit it off. A couple of years later, Bava found employment on an adaptation of the tragic story of *Beatrice Cenci*, a film directed by Freda, helping out with optical effects. Somewhere along the line, the pair dreamt up the idea to make a horror movie. Freda would direct, of course, and Bava would shoot the picture – his pal's ability to work fast was apparently part of Freda's sales pitch. Ermanno Donati and Luigi Carpentieri, the producers, liked the scenario Freda had described to them (the idea was expanded upon by Piero Regno and J.V. Rhemo) and approached Goffredo Lombardo of Titanus. The project was given the go-ahead. British film critic and broadcaster Alan Jones noted that Mussolini's banning of horror titles in previous years produced a potential opportunity in the market: '*The fact that these famous classics were finally shown on Italian shores during the early 1950s might actually have been the impetus for Freda and Bava to consider delving into the much-maligned fantasy field in the first place*' (2013: 22).

I vampiri, much like *Black Sunday* four years later, differed from the traditional vampire picture. Vampirism, here, was depicted from a cod scientific angle and related to the theme of ageless beauty, eternal life and the sheer narcissistic anxiety of losing one's looks. Stacey Abbot highlighted the film's modernism in her online article for Kinoeye (2002): '*In particular, I vampiri modernises the vampire legend by presenting vampirism as a product of the modern world rather than an opposition to it long before the presence of a vampire within a contemporary setting became the standard*.'

The plot is delivered in the mystery-thriller style with interruptions of Gothic atmosphere. An intrepid and mightily determined reporter, Pierre Mantin (Dario Michaelis), is set on exposing the dastardly Giselle du Grandan (Gianna Maria Canale), who keeps her youthful looks intact via a serum whose main component is the blood of virgins (from girls who are captured and disposed of once they've been drained of their vital life source).

The crimes of Giselle du Grandan in *I vampiri* were based upon the legend of Elizabeth Bathory who, in 1610 (only twenty years before the initial events of *Black Sunday*), was arrested on suspicion not only of witchcraft, but the murder of hundreds of young maidens of the court and village peasants. Of course she did not soil her own well-manicured hands and murder anybody herself – she had willing lackeys to do the dirty work for her. Countess Dracula (as Hammer would one day call Bathory) believed, under guidance from a local witch, that bathing in blood would stop the ageing process. It didn't. She ended up imprisoned in a castle for the rest of her natural life. Those who aided the crazed aristo were not so fortunate.

Italian Gothic is born in I vampiri

On Day 10 of the allotted 12-day production, Freda walked out. It was said to have been a tense set with the director's attitude described as *'imperious'* by Bava (Lucas, 2007:157). The cameraman and special effects magician stepped up to the plate and reworked the picture working against varying factors such as actor availability and budgetary constraints. Tim Lucas detailed the changes in a DVD commentary for *Black Sunday*:

> Bava's input was especially significant, as it was he who decided to raise the supporting character of the journalist to the lead, dispense with a *Frankenstein* sub-plot about a dismembered criminal reassembled and brought back to life, and flesh out the film with stock footage, montages of newspaper presses and audaciously sustained long-takes.

It would be pushing it to declare *I vampiri* as a neglected masterpiece, but it is a hugely underrated work and very cleverly sets out what a horror film with a modern edge and sensibility could achieve. The unusual angles, shadow play, the dolly shots, deep-focus photography and trick effects would all be found again in *Black Sunday*, although with much more ambition. *I vampiri*'s aesthetic is an *amuse-bouche* compared to the full visual feast served by the latter.

The narrative, quite importantly, does not take place in Italy but Paris, France. The perfume of glamour associated with the City of Lights ramped up the thematic subtext. Paris is the global fashion capital and one of the most quixotic cities in the world. Giselle du Grandan, the wicked vampire at the centre of the storm could reside nowhere else on earth but among the high society of Paris, the classy boulevards and famous fashion houses. Her chateau, however, is more like a Gothic castle than a typically posh Parisian residence. Bava shot all the Parisian street scenes in the courtyard of Scalera Film Studios.

I vampiri showcased Bava's inventiveness from the very beginning via a matte painting/ shot of a distant but still giant Eiffel Tower, with the foreground given over to wasteland and a river. Given the semi-rural look, there's no way this is a convincing portrayal of 1950s Paris in relation to the tower's position. The graphical quality serves as an idiosyncratic interpretation of the city with a cultural landmark plonked down somewhere it could never conceivably viewed from.

A glass matte shot of the Eiffel Tower overlooking a semi-bucolic landscape in I vampiri.

The same occurs later, in another matte shot, where we see the Notre Dame cathedral on the skyline. The picture postcard opening credits sequence, set to Roman Vlad's romantic, doom-laden score, helped in the establishment of a (creaky) foreignness that worked rather like the dreamy and weird paintings of Henri Rosseau (1844–1910). Presumably Bava and Freda hoped audiences wouldn't recognise or care about the phoney use of locations. Yet I can't help but think of the French artist in relation to Bava, here. Whether some wild jungle with a pouncing tiger (Rosseau) or the brooding, fog-smothered painted landscapes of Moldavia (Bava) or an Italian semi-industrial landscape something kindred and uncanny in the exotic visions of both artists.

3. PRODUCTION AND RECEPTION

ROLL CAMERA!

La maschera del demonio began production on 28th March at Scalera Film studios. An intense shoot, it lasted six weeks and wrapped on 7th May. Six weeks was a typical production period for Galatea-backed projects, but quite generous compared to others. Most Italian *filoni*, back then, were given between just two or three weeks to get projects in the can. It was a good year to make and release a picture in Italy, too. 1960 was the 'annus mirabilis' for the industry, where '*the share of domestic box-office for Italian film reached 50 per cent for the first time since the war*' (Nowell-Smith, 1996: 7).

BARBARA STEELE

That face! Those eyes! Barbara Steele, in her breakout role(s) as Asa and Katia, would launch a thousand wet dreams and equally a thousand nightmares. The actress was completely wrong when she claimed anybody could have played Asa and Katia. Nobody but Steele could have played those roles. She admitted the film is a visual work of art but felt discontented with her performances as an actress. That's entirely fair. How she is presented in relation to lighting, shot choices and the general Gothic air is what makes Steele so unforgettable. It is a performance uniquely cinematic. For years, Steele had offered contradictory views about her most famous screen role. She told *Halls of Horror* magazine (1983): '*The thing is, the horrors are the only films one hears about, which is just a frigging drag. I always used to think they'd end up only in Sicily. It's not so. They end up at the Odeon while all the things you did for love and nothing end up in late-night showings at the Tokyo Film Festival!*'

Steele was born in 1937 on the Wirral peninsula in the county of Cheshire. An art student turned actress, she was the very last contract player signed by the Rank organisastion. The company, it has been said, didn't quite know to know what to do with the girl.

By the late 1950s, Steele had appeared in several minor pictures such as *Bachelor of Hearts* (1958) and *Upstairs and Downstairs* (1958) before Rank sold her contract to

Twentieth-Century Fox. Her foray into American cinema was pretty much a disaster and curtailed by her allegedly walking off set after a row with director Don Siegel, a few days into the making of the Elvis Presley vehicle, *Flaming Star* (1960). Steele referred to her time in America as: '*I went to Hollywood and sat on a bench for two years*' (ibid.).

Be warned: the actress has been found an unreliable narrator of her past and career, and with a penchant for getting things plain wrong. For example, she was insistent *La maschera del demonio* was shot in Rome in the dead of winter and that the film's rich monochrome photography was achieved by everybody wearing black and white costumes. This just isn't true. You only have to look at promotional stills taken during the production to see the richly textured lighting and colourful costumes, often velvet, in deep reds and purples. The expressive colour design was exactly what made the black-and-white photography so damn good. Therefore, it is best to tread carefully around her reminisces. Not that they are entirely worthless, far from it, but memory can play games with the mind.

Barbara Steele in the role that would make her a screen icon

Steele discussed an actors' strike (that occurred in March 1960) which allowed her time to abscond to Italy and where she no doubt felt infinitely more glamorous, the place more much cultured and civilised than the dying factory known as Hollywood. Low-budget genre movies are low-budget genre movies no matter where the sound stage happened to be located. '*Fortunately for me, the actors' strike happened. A complete shut-*

down in Hollywood. The studios couldn't pay anyone so we were like free for four months. They couldn't stop you doing anything you wanted to! I went to Italy… and this film turned up' (ibid.).

How Mario Bava cast the peripatetic young actress runs in several versions. The most convincing one is that he picked up stills of Steele that landed on his desk one day from a pile of CVs and headshots often used during the casting process. They had been sent courtesy of the William Morris Agency. The other version, which sounds like a load of baloney, sees Bava captivated by a moody photo-shoot feature featuring Steele in Life magazine that compelled him to track down the actress and cast her as Asa and Katia. (This is Steele's version of events.)

Bava's choice of actress and the role he gave to her showed what Hollywood had failed to notice; its vision of femininity and appeal rather jejune, in comparison. Picture Doris Day next to Barbara Steele as Asa/Katia. Either way, Bava saw a way of utilising the actress in a more creatively rewarding way than as eye candy to prop up rom-coms and melodramas shooting in Los Angeles. Freda, who would cast Steele in his own films, said of the actress: '*They are the eyes of a Chirico painting. Sometimes in certain lighting conditions her face takes on expressions which don't seem human, and would be impossible for any other actress*' (Pirie, 1977: 158).

Steele's ability to appear utterly beautiful, give off threateningly sexual vibes, look melancholic – and even downright wicked – created an extraordinary frisson that served the film so well. One wishes to rewrite and update the final line of Roland Barthes' short essay in *Mythologies* (1957), titled *The Face of Garbo*: 'The face of Garbo is an Idea, that of Steele, an Event.'

Geoffrey McNab, interviewing Steele for *The Guardian* newspaper and website, under the headline 'Barbara Steele: the accidental scream queen' noted what Bava, Freda and others had also seen. '*Steele still has that uncanny, saturnine look and those piercing, deep-set eyes that made her such an unsettling screen presence*' (2011).

Despite a very uneasy working relationship, Bava and Steele – for just this one picture – created something extraordinary. So why did they work together only once? Steele is said to have had a rather snooty attitude towards making a horror film and her temperamental (some say neurotic) nature worried Bava, who later wanted to cast her in *The Whip and the Body*, alongside Christopher Lee, but thought the better of it. Instead, Steele teamed up for several films with Freda and also Antonio Margheriti. She became the face of Italian Gothic. In America, she worked for Roger Corman and AIP. Steele's career, thanks to movies such as *Black Sunday* – especially *Black Sunday* – has remained a source of fascination for fans, critics and academics alike.

OTHER CAST MEMBERS

Cast as the romantic lead/hero (though one hesitates to call Gorobec the hero of the piece) was John Richardson (born 1936, Worthing). He was another former Rank contract player that had headed out to the sunny climes of Italy in search of opportunities. Richardson had been a model and also appeared in *Bachelor of Hearts*, the film that also featured Steele in a minor role. He would later crop up in several 'Hammer Horrors' before swapping acting for a career as a photo-journalist. As Gorobec, he is perhaps one of the least interesting elements of *Black Sunday*. A bland figure (he's even blandly handsome), Gorobec doesn't really have much to do until the end of the second act and into the third, where he plays detective and must stop Asa's infernal scheme from being fulfilled. Katia captures his eye when they first meet in the ruined grounds of the chapel and crypt, but as a hero and a performance, Richardson is hardly memorable.

Dr. Thomas Kruvajan was played by Andrea Checchi (1916–1974) and his voice dubbed by Bernard Grant. Checchi's role as the doomed medical practitioner, it is claimed by Tim Lucas in the *Black Sunday* DVD audio commentary, was modeled on his good pal Bava. The Florentine actor, unlike the young leads, had established film-making calibre having worked with lionised figures of post-war Italian cinema such as Michelangelo Antonioni (*La Signora Senza Camelias*, 1953) and Vittorio De Sica. 1960 was a good year for Checchi as he appeared in Fritz Lang's *The Thousand Eyes of Dr. Mabuse*, the US-German director's swansong.

Andrea Checchi and co-star John Richardson as Kruvajan and Gorobec

Starring as the devoted Karloffian brute Javuto was Sicilian actor Arturo Dominici (1918–1992). Dominici had had a role in the Freda/Bava picture, *Caltiki – The Immortal Monster*. Rounding off the supporting players was Ivo Garrini (Prince Vajda), Enrico Olivieri (Constantine Vajda), Tino Bianchi (Ivan) and Antonio Pierfederici as the priest. Bava gave the minor but important role of Sonya to Dominici's daughter, Germana, whose lonely walk through the dark night to feed Irina the cow in a shed by the cemetery, is one of the film's outstandingly eeriest scenes.

MARKETING BLACK SUNDAY

The marketing campaigns for *Black Sunday* (under all release titles) ramped up the promise of sex and violence. There were plenty of publicity shots of Barbara Steele in provocative poses, both in and out of character(s). The American poster devised a hand-drawn montage within a central panel. The main image depicted Asa's face, in black and white, accentuating those remarkable eyes – those whirlpools of dread – in a style that pre-dated by a good twenty years the panda-eyed goth girl. Asa's hair flows, too, at a peculiar angle (almost horizontal) as if making a playfully satanic reference to Botticelli's *The Birth of Venus*. Below, in colour, is a giant flame, the embers of which contain the torch-bearing crowd of hooded inquisitors. In the middle of the flame, Asa is depicted tied to the wooden plank, the presence of two burly executioners at her side suggesting a borderline S&M scenario. In the far right hand corner, in smaller detail to create a distance between the centre of the poster and the side, Javuto rides his phantom carriage towards the scene. In the far left corner, Prince Vajda sleeps soundly in a coffin. It is a remarkable and beautifully drawn poster that does not skimp on the film's details. A 'quad' version also exists with a majority of the images toned red.

The poster tagline replicates, too, in spirit, what Romantic poet Percy Bysshe Shelley referred to in his poem on a painting of the Medusa (attributed at the time to Leonardo Di Vinci) as the '*tempestuous loveliness of terror; for from the serpents gleam a brazen glare*' (Shelley, 1819: 492). It reads: '*Stare into these eyes, discover deep within them the unspeakable terrifying secret of Black Sunday … it will paralyze you with fright!*'

A warning is also given in a box that reads: 'Please note. The producers of *Black Sunday* recommend that it be seen only by those over 12 years of age!' Interestingly, the US trailer ups the age limit by a couple of years with Voiceover Man informing the viewer of the producers' '*moral obligation to warn you that it will shock you as no other film ever has. Because it could be very harmful to young and impressionable minds, it is restricted to those over fourteen years of age.*'

When it was finally released in the UK, in 1968, as *Revenge of the Vampire*, the stark advertising poster used a similar image of Asa, in black and white, though much more crudely done, and also made sure that she had vampire fangs protruding from her lips. Yet again the effect of Steele's eyes are captured in their uncanny glory. The comic book-style 'dripping-blood' font is generic stuff and the tagline lacks the Gothic poetry of the American poster. The tagline boasted: '*The undead demons of hell terrorize the world in an orgy of stark horror.*'

The Italian and AIP trailers made damn sure the blood and guts were repeatedly displayed in teasing fashion. The American promo begins with a reference to Count Dracula: '*Not since Dracula stalked the earth as the world so terrifying a day or night … Black Sunday is unlike any motion picture you have ever seen!*'

The Italian promotional reel is a much classier affair that exclaimed a trio of emotional responses: '*L'orrore*' (horror) '*L'angoscia*' (anxiety) and '*Il terrore*' (terror), before going on to mention, rather poetically, that the film trades in the '*cold language of images*'.

In both formats, trailers and posters marketing the film appeared to be doddle, with the remit: 1. Show off the gorgeous compositions but get across to potential viewers that this ain't no art film 2. Use countless shots of Barbara Steele's hypnotic eyes and heaving bosom and highlight the fear/sex factor. 3. Throw in a few gore shots.

LA MASCHERA DEL DEMONIO BECOMES BLACK SUNDAY

It is entirely wrong to think what AIP did to Bava's movie was a travesty against Bava and the film. In some instances, AIP improved the picture. (I am in agreement with Tim Lucas that the removal of Gorobec's excessive dialogue at the very end, in which he tells the priest his life is over if Katia dies – 'My life is finished too, now!' – was a wise decision.)

Movies have always been cut depending on where they are screened in the world: whether that's studios guided by demographically-focused test screening comments, censorship boards or distributors deciding changes need to be made when marketed to a particular country or audience. We might think movies are universally embraced, but they're not. What works in Birmingham might not work in Bueno Aires. Today, film producer Harvey Weinstein has earned the snarky nickname 'Harvey Scissorhands' due to his penchant for taking foreign movies and cutting them for an American audience. AIP purchased the film from Galatea and gave it more than a trim to suit their own requirements.

We live in an age where various cuts and alternate versions of movies are made readily available. They are often boxed together as 'Special Editions' or 'Anniversary Editions'. Mark Kermode has stated the release of different cuts of the same movie has become more 'obligatory than optional, with no film "finished" any more, at least not the traditional sense' (2013: 155).

There is a mixture of curiosity and anticipation at viewing previously unseen material. The home entertainment market revolutionised access to such things and distributors found, after initial hesitation, they could make even more profit from movies long after theatrical runs. 'Deleted and Alternate Scenes' have become a regular staple of Blu-ray and DVD releases. Movies can no longer speak for themselves: we demand the ephemera, the accoutrements; the interviews, the storyboard galleries, the excised footage and the commentary track. The whole artistic process can now be laid bare to glare at. What was once perhaps an exclusively academic concern (foraging around archives for material) has become an ingrained part of movie fandom.

Simon Rowson in 2011 discovered in the National Film Centre, outside Tokyo, the surviving reels of a 35mm *Dracula* (1958) print. Damaged by a fire in 1984, the first half of the movie was toast but reels 6, 7, 8 and 9 remained intact. From these Rowson was able to identify two 'extended scenes' cut out of the British and American prints. The film had been restored by the BFI in 2008 but such was the buzz surrounding the latest discovery that it forced another re-release in 2013. The restoration used an American print which is slightly longer than the British version, though it used the correct – and original – title card, '*Dracula*', and not '*Horror of Dracula*'. Now that we have the scenes of Dracula nuzzling his victim before going in for a pint of the red stuff and the character scratching the decayed flesh from his disintegrating face, do we consider it the 'superior' or even 'best' version? Does it negate all others? This question concerns AIP's released version of the film in English-language territories, which since 1991 has battled with the until then never-before-seen-or-released *The Mask of Satan* cut once rejected by AIP. It must have been quite incredible to watch.

With regards to *Black Sunday*, AIP's sometimes liberal attitude to cutting and shot removal certainly nullified some of Bava's more graceful beats and faded to black during awesomely gory moments (or removed them entirely). The effect achieved, one can dare to say, is akin to a foreign novel being (rather fancifully) adapted into English with the translator's own input altering the text. Given the demands of the industry and other elements, there is just no point whatsoever treating any original release version as sacrosanct.

AIP released their version of Bava's debut feature in the summer of 1961. It was a smash hit for the distributor and earned $14,750 dollars in its first week at the Allen Theater, Ohio, where it premiered on February 3rd 1961. The film was a hit – bigger than Corman's first Poe adaptation, in fact. It took $706,000 in rentals and played in movie houses for years. Would it have been the same triumph if AIP had accepted – without reserve – Galatea's shipped print? The sexual suggestion and violence was just too strong. AIP, it seemed, were a tad more prudish than even the British.

La maschera del demonio *becomes* Black Sunday

During the filming of *La maschera del demonio*, the actors had delivered their dialogue in English, with the exception of Checchi, Domenici and the actor's daughter. A live soundtrack was recorded to provide a rough guide during the post-production dubbing process. Steele once claimed she'd re-recorded her lines of dialogue in New York, but this isn't the case. Joyce Gordon provided the vocals for *Black Sunday*. (Tim Lucas does attest, however, that one of Steele's screams can be heard in the film.) AIP conducted the redubbing sessions at Titra Sound Corporation. As well as certain scenes being altered in the editing suite, the score, dialogue, sound effects and character names were also changed. Andrej Gorobec was now Andreas Gorobec, Choma Kruvajan became Thomas Kruvajan and Igor Javutich became Javuto.

The opening moments of *Black Sunday* furthered the advertising poster's stark warning that children under the age of 12 will not be permitted to see the film. This was achieved by the inclusion of a stagey, even po-faced, pre-credits title crawl accompanied by Les Baxter's booming score: '*The producers of the picture you are about to see feel a moral obligation to warn you that it will shock you as no other film ever has. Because it could be very harmful to young and impressionable minds, it is restricted to those over fourteen years of age.*'

Then something rather wonderful occurs. After the message has crawled off the screen, we are left in darkness … complete darkness and with only Baxter's score to keep us company. This lasts for over 10 seconds. Is this a mimicking of an overture before an opera begins? It is much closer, in fact, to the dreamlike nature of the movies – that empty, unknowable space in between nocturnal reveries. The start of a film is like the start of a dream. Emptiness, then an abrupt flash of light, and we begin! *The Mask of Satan* used a similar but much less effective opening into darkness that lasts only 5 seconds. By extending it, AIP make it feel more pronounced and dreamlike.

How AIP came to purchase the film goes back to the business opportunities American producers saw in genre fodder made in Roman studios. In 1960 Sam Arkoff and James Nicholson were invited by their man in Italy, Fulvio Lucisano, to view a new picture from Galatea titled *La maschera del demonio*. Arkoff related his first impressions in a 1997 article by Tim Lucas titled *Reinventing The Mask of Satan*:

> And then this picture started … It was terrific! We saw it in Italian with an interpreter, which isn't usually satisfactory, but Fulvio would chime in from time to time to make things more understandable. But it was picture of a first-class horror and suspense director. (1997: 57)

Arkoff and his business partner snapped up the rights for $100,000 (or thereabouts). AIP received delivery of a recently prepared English-language cut, titled *The Mask of Satan*, which had been dubbed by ELDA (English Language Dubbing Association) with dialogue directed and written by George Higgins III. It was decided that AIP could not release it in the movie houses of Midwest America with so much savagery on display and certain transgressive moments that would not play well. '*All of AIP's films were very clean so anything that was suggestive of playing around – fornicating a corpse, you know what I'm saying? – we couldn't stand for it*' (ibid: 47).

Did they really not understand Corman's *The Fall of the House of Usher*? With the insinuated incestuous longing for the sister by the brother? The sequence in which Asa tempts Kruvajan into becoming her familiar was botched in the re-edit by AIP and runs with a much more Gothic and erotic feeling in other versions. Kruvajan puckers up for a passionate kiss, but in *Black Sunday* the scene cuts away at the vital moment. AIP believed, too, that having 'Satan' in the title would offend Christian sensibilities.

ROBERTO NICOLOSI & LES BAXTER

Roberto Nicolosi's score was replaced by the work of Les Baxter and thus began an AIP tradition regarding Bava's films they distributed in the USA. Baxter's compositions are definitely – maybe even defiantly – unsubtle. Nicolosi's music (orchestrated by Pier Luigi Urbini) was a quickly produced effort (rather than tailor made) that riffed on Hammer's *Dracula* and featured wind instruments in places. Yet both work well enough if you watch either *Black Sunday* or *The Mask of Satan.* It's simply a matter of European taste versus American. Neither is an overall winner. Also, Baxter's own bombastic opener isn't a world away from Barnard's style.

AIP adjudged that there simply wasn't enough of Nicolosi's arrangements and the film needed a new approach. The score was replaced because Arkoff and Nicholson felt it was simply 'too Italian' and American audiences wouldn't like it. The bombastic James Bernard-like opening theme and the eerie silences of *The Mask of Satan* – which let the images do the talking – were removed in favour of a romantic and sweeping score jam-packed with sometimes monstrously horrendous cues. Just listen to the scene where Kruvajan and Gorobec approach the church pipe-organ in the Vajda ruins for a supreme example of Baxter's occasionally overstuffed style. Elsewhere, it is rather well done.

THE FILM'S RECEPTION

Black Sunday (under any release title) did not take decades to be appreciated. It garnered excellent reviews and very decent receipts. It is fair to say, though, the movie was more a hit internationally than at home. When released it earned 140,000,000 Italian Lira (the figure given by Tim Lucas), which, in dollars, was converted to $87,000. Not exactly what you'd call a stellar return.

Tom Milne, a UK critic, was an early fan of Bava and his debut feature film (which he'd reviewed during its release as *Revenge of the Vampire*). Writing in 1981, for a critical dictionary of cinema, he praised it and the director as '*a superb painter on celluloid*' (1981: 235). For *Monthly Film Bulletin* (August 1968) he waxed: '*One of Bava's best films, with a fluid visual style and a narrative grip that only weakens towards the end. Some chilling moments, of both beauty and terror, he has never surpassed.*'

French critics were champions of Bava's oeuvre in general. Jean-Paul Torok, in his review for *Positif*, which also saw fit to put Steele on the front cover of their July 1961 issue, was ebullient; his review tinged with a sense of the poetic that sounds admirably OTT when translated into English: '*Let a meteoric film burst into a flash of lightning on the horizon, and, one salute it in passing, taking the necessary time to make a wish*' (1961: 57).

Cahiers du Cinema's Fereydoun Hoveyda, in his article 'The Faces of the Demon', noted: '*The camera is extremely mobile, moving around with nostalgic grace that is perfectly fitted to the neo-romanticism of Gogol's story*.' He also commented – much like Milne would do – that '*Bava has the soul of a painter*' (1961: 55).

Release in the UK

Bava's film struggled against the decision-making of the BBFC (the British Board of Film Censors, as it was then known) when submitted by Anglo-Amalgamated (AIP'S UK distribution partner). We know that the film was screened once – as *Black Sunday* – at the National Film Theatre during Christmas 1961 when Tod Browning's *Freaks* was pulled from the schedule. *Black Sunday*, years later in 1986, received a home entertainment release by Stablecane Ltd and awarded the '15' certificate.

In 1991, UK label Redemption Video released a version of Bava's film as *The Mask of Satan*, which quite frankly must have blown the heads off people that had spent the past thirty years watching prints of AIP's cut.

Censorship in the UK

All of Bava's films released in Great Britain would be subject to the '*nannyish British censor, who is carefully removing a large part of his films' raison d'etre*' (Petley, 1982: 33). The BBFC's John Trevelyan commented in his autobiography, *What the Censor Saw*:

> A film called *Black Sunday* was refused a certificate in 1961 on the grounds of disgust, but was eventually passed by the board in 1968 because by this time it looked rather ridiculous. It was then distributed under the title *Revenge of the Vampire*. (1973: 166)

The BBFC rejected the film outright on 10th February 1961. It had been submitted by Anglo-Amalgamated and ran to 86 minutes (7746 feet of film). The cost of submission was £57. The decision, related back to the company in a letter dated 14th February, stated: '*We have run the film* Black Sunday *twice and I now have to write to you to say that we cannot issue a certificate for it. We think that quite a lot of the material in this horror film goes beyond what we consider legitimate for film entertainment, and that it is frankly disgusting.*'

In general, the BBFC examiners did not like it. An examiner's note dated 10th February described it as a 'dull film' (are they supposed to act as critics?) and that it was full of 'disgusting shots and sadistic ones'.

From the handwritten and typed notes I read during a visit to the BBFC, where I was given access to all the files they had on *Black Sunday/The Mask of Satan/Revenge of the Vampire*, there appeared five very clear issues the organisation had with the movie. In a report dated 11th January 1961, the following shots were cited as the main offenders:

Reel 1 – 'Branding of the witch'.

Reel 1 – 'The torture in application of the witch's mask'.

Reel 2 – 'The insects crawling around the decaying face of the witch'.

Reel 5 – 'The extreme close-up of the witch's face in the coffin, showing nail holes'.

Reel 9 – 'The close-up of the father's burning features in the fireplace. Camera returns to this twice'.

The BBFC remained stringent on the matter and cited in several letters back and forth that cutting the picture would not help it gain a certificate for exhibition. What is most interesting is both the American company (AIP) and Anglo-Amalgamated refused to give up at the first hurdle and re-sent prints for the BBFC to view again and again. They seemed somewhere between mildly annoyed and bemused that the BBFC would not pass it for exhibition. But the censors remained adamant: *Black Sunday* would not see the light any projector in the United Kingdom.

In a letter to John Trevelyan dated 22nd February 1961, Anglo-Amalgamated tried a different tactic and argued with the BBFC that *Black Sunday* was passed without much bother in the USA. The friendly tone between the correspondents highlighted that the BBFC did not have a particularly iron-fisted, dictatorial and humourless attitude – they just refused to pass the picture on the grounds that the film was, in their own words, 'disgusting'. Anglo-Amalgamated tried and tried until the unfolding drama lurched into comedy. One letter sent to the BBFC, dated 22nd February, apologised for a mishap: '*American Independent Pictures sent us the wrong print of* Black Sunday. *They are sending us another print which has a production code seal in the United States and has been rated A-2 by the Catholic League of Decency*.'

This went on for months – into the summer of 1961 – before the BBFC refused to hear anything further from AIP or Anglo-Amalgamated. All was quiet until 1963 when New Realm Pictures sought clarification over the matter with the idea that the London County Council would permit the screening of a print they had called *The Mask of Satan*. They contacted the BBFC, seemingly out of politeness and procedure, asking for clarification on potential censorship issues. The BBFC wrote to the London County Council's Public Control Department on 29th October 1963, detailing their opinion: '*The film is a horror film of a particularly unpleasant kind. It is an improbable film which contains elements of black magic, vampirism and necrophily*.'

Bava's debut was by now attracting the attention of cinephiles. The BBFC noted that a publication titled 'Motion' (Issue 4) reproduced '*one of the nastier shots*' on their front cover under the subject matter dedicated to violence in the cinema. Again, the film was refused exhibition on grounds that it was a nasty flick unfit for the masses. By 1968 the judgment of the organisation had changed utterly. Writing to the BBFC, in a letter dated 2nd June 1967, Mrs. Negus-Fancey, at the behest of E.J. Fancey Productions Ltd, asked them to review previous decisions and informed the BBFC the company had '*paid money to Italian producers some years ago and had not been able to get any of it back*'.

The film was again resubmitted, in 1968, as *Revenge of the Vampire*. It was passed for certification on 10th May 1968 and released through Border Films. (The official certificate actually reads: '*Revenge of the Vampires*'.) This cut – *The Mask of Satan* version with a new title – now ran at 7732 feet and cost £76 to submit. Two cuts were ordered to be made (and cuts were also ordered from the promotional trailer): the branding of the witch still posed a problem and Reel 5's shot of Asa's decayed torso under her cloak was removed. An examiner's note, dated 3rd May 1968, commented that '*It looks pretty tame now.*'

The news of the film's release caused the Horror Film Club of Great Britain to write to the BBFC in June 1968 enquiring about the examiner's decision. Clearly, there were eager fans out there desperate to see the movie. After seven years Bava's debut – with a new title and minor cuts made – was finally available for big screen distribution.

MARIO AND THE SURREALISTS

Roland Caputo, in his *Metro* magazine essay on *Black Sunday*, commented how the 'surrealist contingent' at *Positif* (writers such as Ado Kyrou, Robert Benayoun and Peter Kral) had enjoyed the film immensely. '*Those of a surrealist persuasion were bound to be receptive to the mix of fantastic, the marvellous and the erotic*' (1997: 56).

Today, whichever version of the film you choose to watch, one thing you will note – that carries through regardless – is that it is consistently incoherent, to the point of being utterly bizarre and achieving what can be read as surrealist gestures (along with those appealing aspects stated above by Caputo). Let's be clear, Bava was not being subversive or ever intended to make a surreal movie. Yet the lack of attention to narrative detail and the dialogue, imaginary religious ritual and iconography and character motivation makes Bava's debut, at times, comically weird to the point where it is wide open to ridicule and akin to a film rendition of the old game Exquisite Corpse. An entire alternative monograph could be written purely on its inconsistencies. Laughter is not forbidden or hurtful because some of it is deserved. But elsewhere the garbled and contradictory nature of the film brings febrile, dreamlike results. Along with the sheer erotic charge of imagery, there are so many odd beats and deliciously weird moments to savour.

Kruvajan knocking over a set of church organ pipes is immediately followed by the wheel of a broken down carriage to collapse. Now, the noise might have scared the driver to drop the wheel as he fixes the thing, but the swiftness in the cutting can suggest simultaneous action and that the characters – investigating the Vajda chapel ruins – have entered a place where the influence of magic abounds: the crossing from one reality to another. Asa is condemned as a vampire but is set to be burned at the stake like a witch; but then, due to a rain storm, is placed in the family crypt. Kruvajan suddenly pulling a concealed revolver out of his jacket to kill a giant vampire bat he has failed to splat with his cane is prime surrealism. That he shoots it dead then smashes the flying rodent in anger against the tomb (breaking the glass) also provided a major plot point.

It goes on: the fact the Vajda family do not appear to recognise the portraits hanging in their grand hall are that of Asa and Javuto, despite their prominent place. Javuto is Asa's servant and yet his proud portrait and smock embroidered with the Vajda crest adorns the wall. Trap doors open of their own accord. The innkeeper's daughter watching Javuto's phantom carriage ride only for her to turn up in the bushes to witness Kruvajan talking to the resurrected ghoul (again, for the purpose of a narrative point later on). Asa has the ability to explode the tomb wide open and beckon her servant to rise from the grave, but cannot get up and walk about. Yes, Bava's film is packed with little moments of peculiarity you could mock or enjoy. The choice is yours.

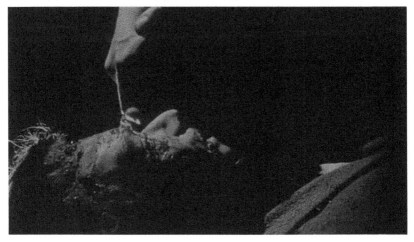

A scene cut from Black Sunday shows Kruvajan's gruesome death in side profile close-up

It is well worth noting, too, that *Black Sunday* features a scene of an eyeball being punctured, which, in my mind, is the ultimate surrealist assault equal to Andre Breton's manifesto declaration about firing a revolver randomly into a crowd. AIP of course rejected the shot but the intent is loaded with repulsion via the priest's line: '*A stake through his eye … as the inscription said.' The Mask of Satan* cut shows the stick thrust into Kruvajan's eyeball and his pained sigh.

Asa's eyes, too, are also remarkable and given plenty of attention – whether filled with gelatinous matter and crawling with scorpions or representing hypnotic power. Ah, cinema and eyeballs! '*Eyes are vulnerable*,' wrote Gilbert Adair. '*Film is vulnerable. And it's the confrontation of two such vulnerabilities which makes the cinema so moving a medium*' (1996: 12).

4. INFLUENCES & ADAPTATION

INTERTEXUALITY

Black Sunday is a fairy tale with an occasional emphasis on the grim and is rife with references, both literary and cinematic. Some are obvious, some less so. As Tim Lucas has pointed out Bava's use of visual quotations – mostly of American horror films – is quite remarkable because of the ban until the early 1950s. Bava was knowledgeable in art history and this definitely shows up in his debut.

> *The director found and drew inspiration from a variety of other artistic sources: Byzantine art, Russian orthodox iconography, fairy tale illustrations, art nouveau, rococo, Disney – and somehow blends believably together in its baleful wash of black-and-white cinematography* (Lucas 2007: 319).

Bava also reworked trick photography he'd used making *I vampiri*. The transformation of Giselle, as she ages before the eyes of the hero, much to her own angst and disgust (vampires, it must be said, are among the most vainglorious screen monsters) was used again, when Katia is drained of her life source by fiendish ancestor Asa (the split screen work is excellent). It was also repeated again, when Asa feels the flames of the smoking pyre licking at her feet and cloak. It was also repeated as Asa feels the flames of the smoking pyre licking at her feet and cloak. Also taken from *I vampiri* was the secret-passage-way-accessed-via-a-fireplace detail. The Vajda crypt is connected, rather handily, via a previously concealed passage behind the grand fireplace! Javuto can move freely between spaces and the machinations of the story to function without too much jumping around between locales. Javuto's hands coming into shot from beneath a mound of freshly disturbed earth referenced a scene in *Caltiki – The Immortal Monster*, where Arturo Dominici's doomed character appeared on screen for the first time. Directors usually wait a while before referencing their own work, but Bava did it in his first officially credited movie.

HORROR MOVIES OF THE 1930s

One of the more immediately noticeable citations is the Universal horror-esque inclusion of torch-bearing peasants, who appear in the film's opening and closing scenes of James Whale's *Frankenstein* (1931). Both Tom Milne and Tim Lucas noted how Javuto's lumbering gait was inspired Karloff's monster too. Asa's crypt and the chapel ruins – with their deeply tenebrous shadows and giant cobwebs – referred back to Karl Freund's photography and the set design of Browning's *Dracula* (1931). The scene in which Prince Vajda sees the Mask of Satan reflected in his goblet is a direct quote from *White Zombie* (1932).

LA BELLE ET LA BÊTE

Arguably one of the most – if not *the* – strongest stylistic influence on Bava is Jean Cocteau's adaptation of *La Belle et la Bête* (1946), from the story by Jeanne Marie Leprince de Beaumont. (The influence of the classic fairy tale on another Bava film, *Kill, Baby … Kill!*, has also been duly noted by critics.) While Barbara Steele, in her in dual roles as Asa and Katia, instantly brings to mind the likes of Elsa Lanchester in *The Bride of Frankenstein* (1935) and Kim Novak in Hitchcock's *Vertigo* (1959), Jean Marais played the character Avenant and the Beast (and also the prince who bears a resemblance to Avenant at the end of the movie). Steele, however, played Beauty *and* the Beast! The use of doubling (the same actor in several roles within the same film) is a marvellous surrealist device with which to produce an air of unreality. Whether it's Asa running through the Vajda castle corridors or the father's trek through the dark and lonely woods, during a violent storm, the film definitely informed Bava's debut.

Cocteau also provided Bava with an artistic guide in how to present actors in relation to their surroundings (the sets) and photographic compositions for maximum visual impact. These elements – along with sleek camera movements, often dolly shots – lend the film, at certain points, a poetic dash and make its (countless) flaws totally forgivable. Javuto's slow motion carriage ride, it has been said, was inspired by Belle's entrance into the Beast's castle, yet this moment recalls, too, the scene in *Nosferatu* (1922), where Count Orlok's coachman (played, like Orlok himself, by Max Schrek – another example of cinematic doubling) arrived to pick up Hutter (though the effect was opposite – under-cranking the camera produced a speeded up image).

BRITISH GOTHIC & DRACULA (1958)

Hammer Films' reinvention of Gothic horror laced with a flagrant eroticism had a profound effect. Ivan Butler summed up the British company's output and their appeal as a combination of '*horror, beauty and the ludicrous in about equal proportions*' (Butler, 1979: 17). Kim Newman also noted how 'Hammer Horror' '*treated the "normal" characters and the audience as innocent bystanders in a private battle between the forces of Good and Evil*' (1988: 28).

Hammer's winning mix of high-'stake' dramas and low necklines became a staple of British horror cinema and ultimately a cliché. Bava's film followed the path laid out by Hammer, in certain regards. Barry Forshaw describes Italian Gothic as a '*distinct, strikingly staged simulacra of British Gothic*' (2013: 23).

Leonard Wolf summed up the literary style in his introduction to a reprinting of *Dracula* around the time of Francis Ford Coppola's adaptation. In it we can see the elements often found in Gothic horror movies.

> Characteristically, the Gothic novel has as its protagonist a beautiful and genteel young woman who is pursued by a tall, dark villain who has darkly erotic evil on his mind. The reader follows her flight and his pursuit through a variety of ominous places: ruined castles, noisome caves, prison cells, vaults, sepulchers, monasteries and convents. There are rooms with trapdoors, secret passageways, portraits that leave their walls and walk, animated skeletons, and talking ghosts. Usually, but not always, the heroine is saved from what is usually a fate worse than death by the heroic efforts of a young, handsome, sexually unthreatening man. (1993: 2)

The famed Berkshire-based production outfit built their most enduring and famous film series' on two classic 19th century novels by Mary Shelley and Bram Stoker. From the beginning it had been Hammer's policy to '*Capitalise on subjects and characters that were pre-sold to the public either through radio and television or via myth and legend*' (Cook, 2007: 180).

What better figures to do this with than Frankenstein's monster and a certain bloodsucker from Transylvania? Hammer would act in the same monetary-guided manner as Hollywood and made countless films featuring the dreaded Count Dracula until he supped his last pint of blood – and Dr. Frankenstein created his final monstrosity – in the early 1970s.

As with the Italian films, Hammer's success on the international scene was aided by the material appealing to American distributors and studios. The drive-ins and fleapits of US cities, with their double bill programmes, played an immense role in the growth of what would today are labelled as cult movies. Hammer's films very often received a mixed critical reaction. *The Observer*'s C.A. Lejeune (cited in *101 Horror Movies You Must See Before You Die*, 2009), stated that *The Curse of Frankenstein* (1957) was '*among the half-dozen most repulsive films I have ever encountered*' (97).

Nevertheless, the introduction of high-born and prim Victorian ladies attracted to pleasures of the flesh; buxom tavern wenches; mad doctors; sexy villains, all with their plummy cut-glass RP accents and occasionally regional voices (usually the peasants and barkeeps), and ever more daring insinuations that link those twin pillars of corporeal and spiritual torment – eroticism and death – were essential to the rebranding of Gothic. These driving-force themes were portrayed with a vigour not quite seen before even if, ultimately, films such as *Dracula* had a rather conservative view of the world and an unadventurous moral stance to impart. But at least the public could engage with sometimes saucy material and swoon at the sexy evilness on show. Dracula's sexual menace was naughty stuff, for sure, but safely within the confines of permitted depictions of carnal matters.

Terence Fisher's film was a hit with Italian audiences and very much guided Bava's insistence on English leads. *Dracula* is a masterwork of economy and invention thanks to Jimmy Sangster's screenplay, and *Dracula* came to revolutionise – because of budgetary demands – certain aspects of vampire genre lore. That bloodsucking fiends of the night can turn into animals is referred to by Van Helsing as a 'common fallacy'. What an ingenious way to get around the book's transformation from man into beast! The scene in which Peter Cushing's Van Helsing dictated the habits and abilities of the undead into his gramophone device set the ground rules for many to follow. But not Bava!

Placing Black Sunday in a historical milieu

Opening the film in the year 1630 – and setting the story in the principality of Moldavia – did two things. Firstly, it placed Bava's film right in the centre of the witchcraft hysteria that had swept across Europe, especially, in the 17th century. Jesus was the '*antidote to evil*' (Nugent, 1983: 35). This was an age when superstition and the supernatural were taken very much more as ontological fact than as invention or reflection of folk culture. Black masses, sorcery, poisoning, ritual and human sacrifice and naked frolicking and orgies in the moonlight provoked a very real and palpable sense of terror..

Fear and suspicions of aristocrats or people with perceived magical powers goes back to the likes of Gilles de Rais and would feed into the popular imagination. What *do* they get up to in their castles? Elizabeth Bathory's crimes, too, were committed a mere twenty years before *Black Sunday* begins. Catherine Monvoisin's supposed black magic shenanigans were also causing concern and intrigues in Paris. The Inquisition effectively invented European witchcraft as another powerful and misguided tool with which to persecute and counter other ideologies and religious preferences. Between the years 1643-47, Matthew Hopkins was the scourge of East Anglia in his self-appointed role as The Witchfinder General. A few decades later (1692–1693) the Salem Witch Trials took Church-affiliated paranoia and misogyny to the New World. It would all be so comic were it not for the bloodshed and thousands of innocents sent to the gallows or stake on bogus charges. Asa of the House of Vajda fits right into the historical milieu as a bad aristo that the local peasants and the Inquisition saw fit to destroy.

Moving *Viy*'s Ukrainian setting slightly to the west also edged it closer to Count Dracula. If you thought 'Moldavia' was some made-up Hollywood-like 'Ruritania' – think again. It's very much a real region, part of modern-day Romania, whose territory begins east of the Carpathians and spreads out all the way to the Dniester (a river) of the Ukraine. Transylvania is right next door. Jonathan Harker, in the novel *Dracula*, described his impression of the land (entirely based on Stoker's research in the British Museum library) in his journal as: '*One of the wildest and least known portions of Europe*' (Stoker 1897: 1). It also had a reported vampire problem back in the day. In the *Gazette française*, 26th October 1770 (cited in *Vampires*, 1991), we get this:

> The madness of Vampires, which caused such a sensation in Hungary many years ago, has just broken again in a little town on the borders of Moldavia, accompanied by events which are as horrible as they are bizarre. The plague having entered the town, a few imposters persuaded some of the lower class of persons that a sure way of keeping the contagion under control was to tear out the teeth of the plague-ridden corpses and suck the blood out of the gums. This disgusting practice caused many people to perish, despite the care that the Police took to prevent it from taking place. (35)

The Vajda family's emblem/crest – a dragon – as seen in the fireplace, the crypt and upon Javuto's costume also aligned *Black Sunday* to the historical and very real voivode, Vlad III, also known as Vlad the Impaler, who belonged to the Order of the Dragon. It has been suggested Javuto was a knight of the Order of the Dragon (perfect cover for a Satanist, then). This makes the costume given to his character more historically resonant than AIP's redubbed dismal of him as Asa's 'bitch', to use a modern phrase.

Kruvajan's speech in the crypt, too, is an echo of Count Dracula's speech to Harker about the family past and its glories.

> Ah, young sir, the Szekelys – and the Dracula as their heart's blood, their brains, and their swords – can boast a record that mushroom growths like the Hapsburgs and Romanoffs can never reach. (Stoker, 1897: 26)

> Kruvajan: *'Nothing remains of the ancient princes of Vajda but the dead shadows of their former glory. I think all the Vajdas have disappeared and with them all the history of ancient Moldavia.'*

FAITHFUL ADAPTATIONS

Screen adaptations can prove a bone of contention. If the author has been a long time dead then there's less brouhaha and claims of sacrilege. Many, many times we hear people declare that a film 'wasn't as good as the book'. The best adaptations don't even try a wholesale transference from page to screen. Should *Black Sunday* be viewed as an adaptation of Nikolai Vasilievich Gogol's short story, *Viy*, at all? It very bears little resemblance to the source material, on first appearances, but did provide Bava with some ideas to express in his film.

Viy had been adapted by Wladyslaw Starewicz in 1918, incorporating live-action and animation techniques. When Bava approached Galatea with the idea, it is said Nello Santi was interested because it was based on the work of a respected author. Whether there was a script or no script has been discussed plenty of times with those who worked on the film saying there was and there wasn't. As well as Gogol's short story, Alexis Tolstoy's *The Family of the Vourdalak* (published in 1884) and Bram Stoker's short story, *Dracula's Guest* (1914), may well have influenced Bava. Even Dostoyevsky has been cited as an influence. Bava was a vociferous reader of horror stories and would go on to adapt the *Vourdalak* in 1963 for the anthology feature, known in the English-language version as *Black Sabbath*.

GOGOL'S VIY

Gogol's *Viy* used a fictional folk legend to draw the reader in and created a folkloric context to the story.

> Viy is a colossal creation of folk imagination. This name is applied by people in Little Russia to the chief of the gnomes, whose eyelids reach the ground. The whole story is a popular legend. I did not wish to change it in any way and tell it almost as simply as I heard it. (1835: 151)

In *Black Sunday*, the imaginary folkloric tradition of that unholy day aligned itself very well with Gogol's own invented creature. Whether the dubbing crew knew of Gogol's story is unknown. The device, inventing a mythology/back story, can be seen in countless found-footage movies such as *The Blair Witch Project*'s (1999), with its elaborate and pioneering use of internet marketing, or even the Coens' *Fargo* (1996), which implemented a 'true crime story' milieu to give the heroine and the plot a mundane believability and grounding. 'Based on' is a beguiling tool in fact and fiction. The actual credit on both *The Mask of Satan* and *Black Sunday* announced 'From a tale by Nikolaj Gogol'.

Bava would terrify his children with *Viy* at bedtime and it was clearly very much in his thoughts when deciding upon what to shoot for his debut feature. Gogol's world of haunted beauty and magic is definitely the milieu of *Black Sunday*, even if the treatment of each element would be more Mediterranean than Eastern European in design and flavour.

Viy was originally published in a two-volume collection known as *Mirgorod* (titled after the district in which Gogol was born) in 1835. *Viy* begins with a note from the author informing the reader the monster to who the story lends its title is a folk legend in rural Ukraine (quoted previously). *Black Sunday* begins in a similar sort of vein.

Three university scholars, Khoma Brut, a philosopher, the theologian Khalyava and rhetorician Tiberiy Gorobets finish school for the summer and head off home, journeying together along the open road. Bava took the names Khoma Brut and Khaliava and merged them into one character: Choma/Thomas Kruvajan. Gorobets became Gorobec. There is, however, another association provided by a Cossack character, named Yavtukh, who provided the name basis for Arturo Dominici's Javuto (and Igor Javutich in the other films). The 'iron face' of Viy gave Bava a central and potent visual image to riff on, even if the mask in the film was fashioned from bronze.

Growing weary and realising they might have to spend the night out in a field, the trio seek shelter at a village they come across in the dark. An elderly lady invites them to stay but separates them. Khoma is then pounced on by the host, who turns out to be a witch-vampire after a wee dram of blood. Thus begins a bizarre sequence in which Khoma and the old crone, having jumped on his back and refusing to let go, run around the countryside until the fiend gives up and seemingly expires from sheer exhaustion. She then turns into a gorgeous young maiden right before Khoma's eyes.

After this strange ordeal, the disturbed young man returns home but is forced back to the village. He is informed that the dying girl was found in a weakened state and it was her very last wish on earth that Khoma read the Psalms over her body – as is the ritual – for three nights. Khoma, sensing trouble, is forced to proceed with the request – much against his will – and over the next three nights supernatural events conspire against him. The maiden returns from the dead and calls forth 'King of the Gnomes' Viy, who enters the church wearing his 'iron face' and orders his minions to attack Khoma. The young man dies.

As should be most apparent, none of that sounds remotely like the plot of *La maschera del demonio* or *The Mask of Satan* or *Black Sunday*. So how can it be labelled a faithful adaptation? Bava transplanted the fairy tale atmosphere and malefic tone very successfully. The young and beautiful girl – either willingly or not – corrupted by the devil and the witch-vampire concept (the Russian variation of the witch-vampire was known as an 'eretica') is found in Asa. Also, the following passage from *Viy* highlighted why Bava needed to cast a face that audiences would never forget and one that could give off two very important vibes at the same time.

> A shudder ran through his veins: before him lay a beauty such as there had never been on earth. It seemed that facial features had never before been assembled into such sharp yet harmonious beauty. She lay as if alive. Her brow, beautiful, tender, like snow, like silver, seemed thoughtful; her eyebrows – night amid a sunny day, thin, regular – rose proudly over her closed eyes, and her eyelashes, falling pointy on her cheeks, burned with the heat of hidden desires; her mouth – rubies about to smile … Yet in them, in these same features, he saw something terribly piercing. (ibid:171)

Bava understood *Viy*'s plot could be harvested for its seductive and spooky eroticism and key ideas rather than transcribing the plot from print to screen.

THE FOUR-PAGE TREATMENT

By virtue of an extant four-page story treatment, dated September 1st 1959, we can see the first roots of the project take shape and see how the concept changed dramatically. The treatment was translated and reprinted in Lucas' Bava tome and is very different from what ended up on the screen and included a modern day setting and more overt references to Gogol's *Viy*.

It begins with a married couple lost in the woods as darkness falls and coming across a series of ruins. '*At the edge of the clearing, there's an old church, also in ruins, from which a faint pipe-organ sound is heard. The couple, intrigued, enters the church. The doors and stained-glass windows are literally covered in a frieze of petrified monsters*' (2007: 285).

Attracted by the sound of whistling (just like Messrs Kruvajan and Gorobec hear), the couple encounter a little man who relates to them the story of a Roman centurion's daughter who would turn from a beautiful maiden into an old witch. '*During the night, however, this lovely girl took the form and the character of a witch and went out performing all kinds of spells, harassing people*' (ibid.).

The witch one day meets a philosopher named Choma and becomes infatuated with him. So annoyed is he by the witch's presence and haranguing, he beats her death. The centurion asks Choma, not knowing that he has killed his daughter, to perform the funeral rituals, as per her request. Choma reluctantly agrees and undergoes a barrage of supernatural terror as the witch summons demons and devils to torment the man. On the third night, the creature known as Viy appears and Choma dies from fright. The little man narrating the tale informs the young couple that since that very night no religious ceremony has ever been performed in the church. In a shock twist, the man turns to his wife and notices that she has changed completely. She calls him by the name 'Choma' and bites his neck, in the manner of a vampire. The pair, a young couple in love, felt themselves drawn to the ruins in order to re-enact their immortal spectacle. It was all a pre-programmed drama.

The use of a curse, a centuries-old drama and a terrible fate are major plot points of *Black Sunday*. How Kruvajan became involved and instigated Asa's resurrection is never really commented upon.

It is worth noting the irony of a character, a learned man who, given his education, might not believe too much in whispered tales of ghosts and witches, kicks off the supernatural shebang when he cuts his hand trying to remove the mask from Asa's face after killing a giant bat and smashing up the tomb. '*That's strange. Usually bats shy away from human beings,*' says Gorobec. Indeed, it is strange and another insinuation that malevolent forces have already stirred. Why does Kruvajan feel so compelled to remove the mask? In the AIP version, however, Kruvajan is less devoted to the empirical evidence versus superstition debate when he tells Gorobec '*Science hasn't solved every riddle, my young friend.*' AIP robbed him of a resonant and macabre line when he tells the innkeeper's daughter that she has no reason to fear going to milk the cow in the shed by the haunted cemetery for '*Now, you mustn't be afraid of the dead, they sleep very soundly.*'

In *Black Sunday*, he brushes off the girl's concerns with a smiling assurance: '*They can't hurt you.*'

We might see the two doctors as a luckless pair in the wrong place at the wrong time and punished for their inquisitive nature. Kruvajan also commanded the driver to take the shortcut to Mirogorod – which he is afraid to take – and thus passing the old ruins of the chapel where Asa rests. Was this all destined to happen, given Asa's powerful curse? This makes Kruvajan less a stranger to the scene and more a pawn in a pre-determined game of Good versus Evil. His entire role in life is to wake Asa with a few drops of his blood and become her helper. Perhaps, and allow me to be fanciful for a moment, one of Dr. Kruvajan's ancestors was among that crowd at the beginning of the film, covered by a gown, holding a torch aloft and keen to witness an execution?

We know, too, that Kruvajan is *au fait* with local folklore and the Vajda family history. Is the doctor acting as a pre-programmed sentinel? They become embroiled in the family drama by virtue of their Nosey Parker status, but maybe, too, pushed by cosmic forces and therefore 'chosen'. Really, Gorobec is the only character who is an outsider and a dramatic agent that can alter the course of Asa's plot. He represents, too, the Hammer definition of the ordinary figure trapped in a battle of Good versus Evil.

DRACULA'S GUEST

Published in 1914, a couple of years after the Irish author Bram Stoker had passed away, *Dracula's Guest* has been described as an excised chapter from the famous novel and/or an entirely separate short story based upon Stoker's original notes.

A young man travelling from Munich to Bistritz, at the behest of Count Dracula, on the eve of Walpurgis Night, decides to investigate a ruined village and cemetery. The countryside is darkened (there's a snow storm brewing), the traveller asks Johann, his driver, to stop the carriage and let him walk to a deserted ghost town. The driver and his horses are worried and he describes the place as 'unholy'. The bleak and cold landscapes conjured could heavily recall the gloomy, fog-shrouded world of *Black Sunday* and the scenario in which the man encounters a female vampire in an old ruined crypt, Countess Dolingen of Gratz, and described as a '*beautiful woman, with rounded cheeks and red lips*' brings to mind Kruvajan's doomed meeting with Asa. The setup of a traveller/non-local coming across ruins is very much evident in Bava's original four-page treatment.

THE CURIOUS CASE OF THE FAMILY OF THE VOURDALAK

Bava returned to Russian literature when directing his celebrated anthology picture, *I tre volti della paura* (*The Three Faces of Fear*), released in the USA and other territories as *Black Sabbath*. Accompanying two of Russia's finest literary exports in the film's credits – Tolstoy and Chekov – was French writer Guy de Maupassant. Literary prestige is a wonderful association, but here it was rather blatantly a case of false adversity, if not outright fraud. Bava himself came up with the story for the third act, *A Drop of Water*, and cheekily attributed it to Chekov.

The differences between the Italian release print and AIP's re-edited version are pretty extraordinary and even more extreme than *Black Sunday*. The story order was rearranged, a new introduction filmed, plot details extensively altered, Les Baxter's score replaced Roberto Nicolosi's (something of an AIP tradition), sound effects were changed all together, and the ending – a wonderful piece of counter-cinema that saw Boris Karloff riding a mechanical horse before Bava pulled the camera's focus away even further to reveal the studio set, production crew and the entire artifice of the moment – was missing entirely.

The second story in *Black Sabbath* is based on Alexis Tolstoy's *The Family of the Vourdalak*. The connections between it and *Black Sunday* are intriguing. *The Family of the Vourdalak* is attributed to a less famous member of the Tolstoy clan.

Count Alexis Tolstoy was a cousin to Leo *War and Peace* Tolstoy. He wrote *Vourdalak* in the late 1830s or early 1840s (the exact dates are not known) under the nom-de-plume, 'Krasnorogsky', a name taken from his family's estate, Krassny Rog. One key inspiration in the writing of his own tales of terror was reading Gogol's *Viy*. The writer was said to be obsessed with Gothic stories and wished himself to explore the dark terrain and produce his own ghoulish fantasias. They were not received well at all at first, and *Vourdalak* would not be published until 1884.

Tolstoy had written his vampire tale in French, a sophisticated move entirely in keeping with his upbringing, education and high-ranking status in society. For some critics at the time he was seen as a poseur. Alexis Tolstoy died in 1875, having suffered an overdose of morphine.

The Saint Petersburg journals were sarcastic about what they considered to be his dilettante interest in such things, attributing his work to 'over-indulgence in opium'; but other reviewers were later to see much more in Tolstoy's folkloric tales, and to think that they presented 'an amazingly complex, fantastic design on a canvas of commonplace reality' (1992: 253).

Christopher Frayling considers *The Family of Vourdalak* as one of the very greatest of vampire stories. '*Tolstoy succeeded in fusing the sexual allegory of vampirism (represented in the story by Sdenka's transformation) with the folklore of the peasants who have more 'commonplace' concerns*' (ibid: 253).

An aristocrat and diplomat, Marquis D'Urfe, recounts a wild tale set in a distant part of the Austro-Hungarian Empire (today's Serbia). It begins years after the event, in the drawing room of a palace, after guests have grown tired of talking politics. The man wishes to entertain his guests with an unusual personal experience he'd once had in exotic southern Europe, a place where bandits roamed … along with the undead.

D'Urfe tells how he came across a village in which the father of a family has been absent having decided to go off and hunt down a notorious criminal gang led by a man named Ali Beq. The father, named Gorcha, has given his sons Georges and Pierre orders that, if he returns after an allotted ten days, then he is no longer a human being but a '*vourdalak*', the local lingo for 'vampire'.

Gorcha returns bloodied and moody, but assures his brood that he is well enough and just a bit tired from his adventures. D'Urfe, however, is suspicious. The old man is permanently grouchy and prone to wandering off at unusual hours. As the fractious drama strains the family dynamic further, D'Urfe, now having fallen in love with Gorcha's daughter Sdenka, must continue on with his diplomatic journey.

The finale of Bava's original four-page treatment invokes aspects of *Vourdalk* as much as *Viy* and the cursed family is also a central theme of the story. As mentioned earlier, a thematic motif that crops up several times in Bava's filmography is family betrayal and woes. *Vourdalak* boasted a romantic hero protagonist, who we assume doesn't give rise to thoughts of the supernatural – such stuff is for peasants, not learned men. The Marquis D'Urfe is very much like dashing Gorobec at the centre of a great mystery.

As in Bava's celebrated film, the vampire chooses to attack his own kin rather than pick off strangers or buxom barmaids or frigid upper-class belles. D'Urfe explains that: '*The vourdalak, mesdames, prefer to suck the blood of their closest relatives*' (ibid: 257).

The nature of the curse very much implies events will not cease until either the family is destroyed or an intervention restores order. In *The Family of the Vourdalak* D'Urfe flees in utter terror during a finale that could be described as 'madcap'. Fortunately for the Vajdas and the villagers in *Black Sunday* order is eventually restored. Tolstoy wasn't in such a charitable mood to give D'Urfe a happy ending in which he and Sdenka survive the horrific scenario. We're left with a frightening chase and descent into madness whereupon the hero, on horseback, rides like the wind as a clan of nosferatu (nosferati?) leg it after him. The unkempt forces of the supernatural roar in full effect.

The theme of doubling is present in *Vourdalak*. D'Urfe is convinced a former flame, the Duchess de Gramont, bears a striking resemblance to Sdenka, the Serbian girl he falls in love with – much like Gorobec with Katia, and almost as instantaneously. '*I am not among those, mesdames, who believe in love at first sight of the kind which novelists so often write about; but I do believe there are occasions when love develops more quickly than usual*' (ibid: 265).

Tolstoy goes further to cement the idea of doubling, mentioning '*Sdenka's strange beauty, her singular resemblance to the Duchess de Gramont*' (ibid.).

5. ANALYSIS

Bava's debut feature film is considered to be among the most stylish horror films ever made and won praise for its delicious look and cinematography. The *mise-en-scène* is ravishing – marrying fairy tale to surrealist irrationality – and special effects design, at times, ingenious. John Landis described Bava's directorial skills with a crude American idiom: '*Making chicken salad out of chicken shit*' (Landis, Operazione Paura).

Writing in 1981, Tom Milne summed up Bava's film (noting all its release titles) as: '*A chillingly beautiful and brutal horror film*' and '*atmospherically the film is superb, a chiaroscuro symphony of dank crypts and swirling fog-grounds*' (1981: 235).

Producer Nello Santi initially wished to shoot in Technicolor. Sticking to his guns, Bava filmed on monochrome stock and delivered what is touted as the last great black-and-white Gothic horror picture. An American producer named Lawrence Woolner actually approached Bava in the late 1960s with the proposal to remake a colour version of *Black Sunday*. The project never came to pass although the director is said to have entertained the idea.

Katia's introduction is one of the most gorgeous dolly shots in the film

The simple fact of the matter is the film would not have worked so well if shot, printed and exhibited in colour. The clever effects and use of miniatures, matte paintings,

63

grotesque character transformations and the painted backdrops would have been laid bare. In black-and-white, these elements fused together to create a magical air. The film's clear artifice married to the Gothic tone and fairy tale sensibility lend *Black Sunday* the greatest visual power. If it had mimicked the palette of Hammer, say, the magic and atmospherics would have been irrevocably lost. The black-and-white photography is utterly spellbinding, in places. Take, for example, the scene in which the Innkeeper's daughter goes to milk the cow … how the mood can change so suddenly: the soft welcoming light of the inn fades away (along with the voices of raucous patrons getting steamed on vodka) and deep tenebrous shadows take over. Space becomes tight and the world is suddenly loaded with menace. Although Sonya is mere yards away from the inn, a creepy ambience takes control and the whole time the low angle dolly shot has focused on the young girl's hesitant face as the space closes in around her. The framing is masterful.

Shot on 35mm, using a 1.66:1 aspect ratio, Bava storyboarded his debut feature (a move Tim Lucas noted was unusual for the time) and is credited with photographing the picture. The decision to pre-visualise the film, even if the script was in a continual state of flux, showcased how strongly Bava favoured imagery over the concerns of telling a story, let alone constructing the machinations of the plot. Ubaldo Terzano served as camera operator but it is also said he lighted the picture and the film's look was achieved through collaboration between director and assistant. Bava stated his debut was '*Filmed entirely with a dolly because of time and money, the photography in a horror film is 70 percent of its effectiveness; it creates all the atmosphere*' (Jones, 2005: 62). He also claimed that it would take all of seven minutes to light a shot and twelve minutes to light an entire room.

Shot on soundstages to allow the director full advantage and control of the elements, outdoor scenes were shot on location outside Rome at a castle in the village of Arsoli, which featured as the Vajda home and around Mirgorod.

BAVA'S APPROACH

Ennio De Concini, Mario Bava, Mario Serandrei (the film's editor) and Marcello Coscia all contributed to the story. *The Mask of Satan* and AIP versions listed De Concini and Serandrei as 'Screenplay By'. The editor of the film was no writer but helped Bava shape the film in post-production, so much so, that he earned recognition.

The shooting and editing process is vitally important to understanding how Bava ultimately crafted his picture after shooting. It reveals what could be described as an experimental approach and method which recognised his artistic manner even if the end result was far from perfect. He allowed himself the freedom to alter and rearrange entire scenes and plot chronology. It didn't always work out as scene placement can feel very odd, including the brief moment when Katia appears ever-so-shady in her intent and dialogue – professing that a young girl's eyewitness account of seeing a resurrected Javuto driving a phantom carriage is poppycock. The girl recognises the portrait in the Vajda castle. '*It's only the imagination of a child. Why this man has been buried for over two centuries. Please stop all this will you or I'll go mad.*'

It is an unusual and off-key scene. It has been suggested by Tim Lucas that Bava intended Katia and Asa – at some point in the story previously – to have switched places and this sudden plea for calm and common sense is really a distraction to throw Gorobec and others off the scent. There's something about her smile at the end of the scene, as Constantine asks the good doctor to stay the night at the castle (before the scene cuts away to an exterior locale: a chapel turned mortuary). The line, '*Yes, please do, we'd all feel so much safer*' rings most odd. Clearly, any idea of a switcheroo was abandoned but the jarring scene remained in the final cut. It should be pointed out that Katia is wearing her crucifix under the blouse, which Asa would not be able to stand for a second. So maybe she really is appealing for everybody to be rational in the face of the supernatural? Yet her sudden forthrightness contrasts too much against what we can call her melancholic disposition that is suspicious. Imagine Gorobec all of a sudden gaining a semblance of personality beyond his perfunctory role as the hero? (It would be noticeable.) Katia's stance is a last ditch attempt at common sense and reasoning because if it's all true – as indeed it is – then she will potentially suffer a fate worse than death. She is the archetypal Gothic female figure.

Lamberto Bava, the director's son and also a film-maker, once explained how his father worked in shaping his movies during their actual production or later in the editing room. Improvisation and changes occurred all the time, but it looks very much like he altered quite a lot. Tim Lucas recounted Lamberto Bava's anecdote of how his dad worked in the audio commentary track for *Black Sunday*: '*My father was never satisfied by his stories and he continued to revise them, even after shooting had begun, changing as much as 50 to 60 percent of the script.*' This comment, explaining how his father's worked was backed up by leading lady Steele. '*I never saw a script for Black Sunday. We were given pages day to day. We had hardly any idea what was going down. We had no idea of the end or the beginning either. I'm sure that Bava knew. Maybe he didn't*' (Lucas, 2007: 297).

TECHNIQUE: CLOSE-UPS AND CRASH ZOOMS

The close-up is one of cinema's most unique and powerful tools. A close-up can provide an intense intimacy and detail, and often in horror movies, a sudden electric shock. If Renée Jeanne Falconetti's tears-stained face represented goodness and sacrifice in Dreyer's *The Passion of Joan of Arc* (1928), Steele's role of Asa is the flipside of that – the great sinner whose allure is positively wicked and documented often in close-up. Both Dreyer and Bava fetishised the close-up in their films.

As well as providing shots of Asa's mesmerising fatal beauty, the close-up is deployed to ramp up moments of violence and terror that break away suddenly from the Gothic elegance and replaced with a more modern and daring representation of violence against the flesh. The scene in which Asa and Constantine rush into their father's room to find him stone dead in medium long shot whips a full 180 degrees into a close-up of Prince Vajda's mauled dead face. The suddenness of the camera movement and change of spatial perspective – a real feat of lightning quickness from the camera operator on a customised 35mm camera modified by Eugenio Bava – is one of the film's most frantic and surprising moments. So well applied was the close-up, in particular, that both AIP and the BBFC had grave reservations and issues. It made scenes simply *too* gory. Prince Vajda's immolation in the fireplace was cut heavily by AIP and Kruvajan's death removed entirely.

Kim Newman, in his autobiographical essay on video nasties, 'Journal of the Plague Years', commented very succinctly on why Italian horror films are so damn effective. '*Italian films are staged slowly and with ritual care*' and he goes onto say, '*It is perhaps these meticulous, grand-standing displays of bodily abuse that so upset*' (1996: 141).

There can be no arguing that the stylised violence in *Black Sunday* can nasty. Writer Kier-La Janisse pointed out: '*Bava's movies were not known for their kind treatment of women as much as the fetishisation of violence directed at them*' (Jannise, 2012: 112). This is totally true: the close-up erotises and fetishes Barbara Steele's face in relation to pain and suffering as well as in other scenes, where her deathly beauty enchants.

The Mask of Satan, pounded onto Asa's face by a muscle-ripped lug with a massive hammer, is a startling moment (even if AIP chose a quick fade to black at the moment of impact which removed the sight of bloody tears streaming down the mask's cheeks, a gruesomely poetic touch). The choice of shot, camera angle and sound design combined to potent effect to produce a wince, as we imagine the thick spikes smashing through bone and soft tissue. Of course, it was hardly the first moment horror movies had ever produced such a violent or repulsive image, but had anybody dared open their film in such a spectacularly gruesome fashion? Imagine, if you will, the scene in Hammer's *Dracula*, where upon Van Helsing smashes the stake into Lucy's chest as she lays in her coffin, opening the film rather than occurring towards the end of the second act!

In a video interview included on the Arrow Video Blu-ray release of *Black Sunday*, recorded in Italian, Steele was still impressed by that scene's impact and her part in one of the most sadistic sequences in horror cinema history. '*The first five minutes of* Black Sunday *were incredibly powerful, you know. I'm burned, denounced, there were big men, these executioners all dressed in black, who put on me this mask with these … what are they called … these big thorns in my face. It was an extremely powerful scene in terms of atmosphere … all this before the opening credits.*'

In *Black Sunday* – though more in *La maschera del demonio* and *The Mask of Satan* cut – when spikes hit human flesh blood will spurt wildly all over the place. When a red hot brand marks human flesh, it will bubble and sizzle and leave a lasting mark. Even if softened by editing and discreet fade-to-blacks by AIP, the violence still packs a punch by the sheer insidiousness of how it is presented (photographically, the choice of shots, etc.). AIP deemed certain images and shots permissible (Katia finding Ivan hanging from a noose). Others, not so much.

During the opening sequence, one of the most amusingly grim flourishes *Black Sunday* proffered is the mask held up by the executioner as he walks towards the camera (thus the viewer). The spikes loom ever large. They get closer and closer until the camera – thanks to some nifty editing – looks as if it passes through the eye of the mask and out the other side. For a brief moment, Bava has forced a pseudo-subjective viewpoint onto the spectator. Suddenly our somewhat distant voyeurism is interrupted and takes on an unwanted, more direct, claustrophobic and suffocating gaze.

The crash zoom technique and Italian genre cinema in general go hand in glove. Bava, especially, employed it a lot throughout his career – to the point where it approached that hoary old critical accusation 'self-parody'. Yet in *Black Sunday*, the crash zoom served to heighten the sense of fear and formed a metaphysical symbolism. Like the close-ups, the in-camera effect allowed Bava to express the supernatural and dark magic abilities of Asa and Javuto as they entered or prowled on the edge of a scene. As the camera's focus 'crashes' into an object the detail becomes larger. So if it's a menacing figure, such as the villains in the movie, the dread is increased. Several instances of the zoom effect are used in relation to Asa's awakening, too: often fixed and slowly creeping towards her tomb. When the priest and Gorobec open the coffin in the cemetery, Kruvajan's sleeping face looks unlike the avuncular chap we are first introduced to in the opening scenes. His degradation is complete and the crash zoom is used to register Gorobec's saddened spirit, revulsion and disbelief at the fate of his old friend. When the children find the corpse of Boris by the river's edge, Bava again used the crash zoom to heighten the horror and tension, the man's face caked in mud and blood.

The scene in which Javuto attempts an attack on Prince Vajda strings together a sequence of crash zoom shots in bravura and frenzied succession – some moving forward and some in reverse – so that reaction shots work as a form of dual between the powers of Good and Evil. The mightiest comes as Prince Vajda repels Javuto by brandishing the crucifix. Demon be gone!

SPECIAL EFFECTS

Mario and his father Eugenio were indisputably maestros when it came to visual effects. Bava Jr. used food stuffs – rice, jelly and poached eggs – to make the blood chill. The film is packed with in-camera practical effects, glass matte paintings, miniatures, split screen, clever shot transitions and dissolves, shadow play to suggest off-camera action. To simulate travel and movement, as Kruvajan and Gorobec travel in their carriage, Bava had crew members hold branches and walk them by the window. It's these simple solutions as well as more technically complex designs which so impress film-makers and fans. Bava (and his father) knew their craft inside out.

The chief inspiration for the film's transformation scenes, which suggested life force being drained away, in both *I vampiri* and *Black Sunday*, can be seen in the 1925 version of *Ben-Hur* (dir: Fred Niblo) and Rouben Mamoulian's *Dr. Jekyll and Mr. Hyde* (1932).

> Red grease pencil, invisible on the black and white film stock, and then lit with a red light that concealed the make-up. As the transformation began, the red light was slowly replaced by a green light, giving the appearance of sudden ageing as the make-up gradually becomes visible. Bava enhanced the effect by fitting the actress with a wig made of artificial filaments that photographed white when exposed to direct light. (Lucas, *Black Sunday* audio commentary)

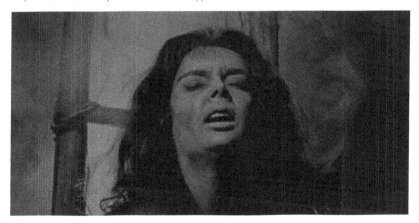

Asa's life force is drained from her body as the flames rise

BEHOLD THE MASK OF SATAN!

Eugenio Bava worked on his son's picture seemingly without ever setting foot on the set. He not only helped customise cameras for the shoot, he sculpted and cast the iconic mask (one was made in bronze) inspired by Gogol's reference to an 'iron face' in *Viy*, as well as other – cheaper – versions of the mask. The finished result appeared suitably medieval but very much unlike the description used by the Ukrainian writer. He also fashioned the 'dead skin masks' of Asa, Kruvajan and Javuto from latex foam.

The Mask of Satan plays a vital function regarding the film's mythology. Masks have been linked directly throughout history with supernatural beliefs, to ward off evil spirits. Is the Mask of Satan a form of death mask too? It is not lifelike, of course, but does it not show the monstrous form under the skin?

'*The true face, the face of Satan,*' Kruvajan tells young Gorobec.

The very first appearance of the mask occurs in long shot as the executioner moves towards Asa with the intention of branding her with the 'S' brand of Satan. We see the mask closer, in side profile, half obscured by shadowy darkness. The cutting and choice of shots is teasing. The giant nose, too, looks very much like an axe embedded straight down the centre of the face. Even these glimpses offer a ghoulish portent.

The Mask of Satan designed by Eugenio Bava

The mask performs several important narrative tasks. The rictus grin, prongs that could well be vampire fangs as well as tusks, bushy eyebrows, flared nostrils and streamlined nose – it runs from an apex at the top of the mask's head straight down the centre of the face to the mouth – make it look carnivalesque and treading a fine line between the comic and the insidious. He should be feared but also mocked as the weaker authority to God. The mask is the essential comic-grotesque depiction of Satan. The designer of the mask, within the world of *Black Sunday*, focused on the bestial and the facial structure brings to mind the goat-like Pan.

Griabe orders his minions: '*Cover her face with the Mask of Satan*.' We then cut to another medium shot of a mask lying at the foot of a tree. This is our first real look at the thing, and in much better light. '*Nail it down!*' commands the Inquisitor.

The mask, as well as functioning as a cruel and unusual torture device, also plays a deeply misogynistic role. Prince Vajda has not only ordered his sister to 'death by immolation' – which doesn't make much sense if she's going to reside in hell anyway and is already, as a vampire, technically dead – but he wants to destroy and deny the woman her own face and substitute it with the mask.

Beyond its use as an instrument of torture and wrecker of beauty, the mask is a supernatural talisman imbued with abilities to ward off evil. Asa, having failed to be burned at the stake due to a thunderstorm and rain lashing down at the exact moment of her death – '*I beheld Satan as lightning fall from heaven*' (Luke, 10: 18) – is placed in the family crypt. They design the tomb with a sheet of glass so that she can symbolically see the mask's reflection for all eternity. Also, as Kruvajan explains to Gorobec: '*They feared that the witch might try to rise again and placed a cross visible to her to stop that happening*.'

FEMALE HORROR ICONS

Female horror icons were few and far between before Barbara Steele's portrayal of Princess Asa. There were plenty of damsel-in-distress roles (Fay Wray in *King Kong*, 1933), but the closest we get, arguably, is Elsa Lanchester's Bride in *The Bride of Frankenstein*. Regarding the latter, yes, the movie title is exclusively devoted to her and the tagline boasted '*The monster demands a mate!*', and Graham Greene's 1935 review for *The Spectator* commented on her '*strange electric beauty*' (1935: 6), but the character's actual screen-time is nothing more than a few minutes leading to the film's explosive and symbolic climax (a phallic-shaped tower is obliterated). With her deliciously camp Nefititi hairdo, balletic movement and svelte patchwork body, the Bride is instantly recognisable but rather jilted by expectation and actually more the bridesmaid to her own film rather than the true focal point, which was still that lumbering and now horny oaf, played by Karloff.

The Island of Lost Souls' Lota the Panther Lady could be another candidate but, again, the film is just not as widely known outside cult cinema confines. Gloria Holden in *Dracula's Daughter* (1936), with her Sapphic longings, is a possibility, but who can truly remember the character … or the film? Could we edge a bet on The Wicked Witch of the West in *The Wizard of Oz* (1939)? Maybe, but it's not a horror film (despite the BBFC's 'A' for 'Adults Only' rating given upon release in 1939). And whilst Hammer's Valerie Gaunt, in the 1958 *Dracula*, showed us the first depiction of a female vampire flashing her pearly white gnashers, the character – although a deeply erotic figure – is nameless and killed off so swiftly as to make hardly any impression at all. None – bar Lanchester – could seriously stake a claim until Steele came along.

Asa

How do you solve a problem like Asa? The answer is: tie the girl to a wooden rack, scar her back with the Brand of Satan, follow that bit of sadism by making her wear the Mask of Satan and then set the body on fire so she may be purified of Lucifer's evil influence by God's righteous fiery element. If only it were that simple…

Asa is a cinematic depiction of a figure often found in Gothic literature and art history known as the Fatal Woman. As Mario Praz stated in *The Romantic Agony*, with an annoyed air of stating the obvious: '*There have always existed Fatal Women both in mythology and literature, since mythology and literature are reflections of various aspects of real life*' (1933: 189).

When Kruvajan is taken to meet Asa in the crypt, her speech, a sales pitch if you will, attempts to convince the doctor there is beauty in death. '*You will die but I can bring you pleasures mortals cannot know*.' Not that he has much of a choice. Yet he succumbs, *almost* willingly.

Fatal beauty: the deathly, voluptuous menace of Asa the witch'

Death and Beauty were '*looked upon as sisters by the Romantics*' and '*became fused as a two-faced herm, filled with corruption and melancholy and fatal in its beauty – a beauty which, the more bitter the taste, the more abundant the enjoyment*' (ibid: 30).

Percy Bysshe Shelley's poetic recounting of seeing a painting of the famed Gorgon in the Uffizi Gallery, Florence, has been described by art historian Praz as a 'near manifesto' for the Romantic concept of Fatal Beauty and of the *femme fatale* which so fascinated the artists, poets and writers of the time. Asa might well be '*La Belle Dame sans merci*' who '*hath thee in thrall*' of John Keats' famed poem.

Praz, too, felt that no other art movement in history had so explored the complexities of Beauty and Death as the Romantics. Shelley would describe the effect of the painting as the '*tempestuous loveliness of terror*' and '*Its horror and its beauty are divine*.' The former could well be assigned as the perfect description of horror cinema's allure and effect. And although Asa is never depicted with wriggling asps in place of locks of hair

(Lamberto Bava's 'remake' of *La maschera del demonio* did make such a reference), she still makes a fine spiritual twisted sister of the Medusa. They are cut from the same cloth. Poor Kruvajan was doomed the moment he entered the crypt!

However, for all its initial radical set-up – a movie about a witch who is dominant, sexy, deadly, and in complete control of male characters and events right up to the finale – when things come a cropper, *Black Sunday* is not a stake in the ground for female empowerment and neither is it forward-thinking enough to let her win. Bava's depiction of the female characters is strictly within the classical confines of art history traditions (Romantic and Gothic) and imbued with the rather dull Catholic and conservative representation of the women in that hoary old 'Saint and Whore' dualism. Asa and Katia can be read, too, as Stoker's Lucy Westenra before and after she's turned into a vampire. Katia is the sweet, pure and unthreatening male ideal of woman – completely and utterly spellbinding in her attractiveness and manners – and Asa is the other side of the coin. '*The sweetness was turned to adamantine, heartless cruelty, the purity of voluptuous wantonness*' (Stoker, 1897: 175).

Two portraits, seen in the film, offer this two-sided depiction of Asa. In the main hall of the Vajda castle, we see her as a young lady of the court and in a secret chamber discovered by Gorobec and Constantine, she is depicted naked and surrounded by satanic objects.

We know next to nothing about Asa. The film begins at the moment of her execution. Given the Moldavian setting and that the character is most definitely wise to the ways of witchcraft, perhaps she attended Scholomance, the legendary private school of the dark arts hidden away somewhere in the mountains of Transylvania?

Asa's punishment might have also been for the transgressing against patriarchal dominance. Did she turn away from her duties and responsibilities as a young lady of the court and grow sexually 'deviant' and against God? Yet the symbolic two fingers up to her father and the other Father is hardly transgressive when seeking an alternate father figure, in Satan. '*He may promise freedom but he is the figure of bondage*' (Nugent, 1983: 10).

Bondage, funnily enough, is the operative word. The very first shot of comely Asa is downright kinky. She is trussed up in ropes, her slender milk-white back revealed by a torn gown with her exquisite legs showing off a fine figure. Let us admire her fine form like that of an ancient statue in a museum or an adult magazine for 'niche' tastes. The effect is the same, either/or. In not showing her face immediately, the camera forces attention directly on the glimpses of flesh and the shape of the body in torn rags. See how the light bathes her right calf and slender shoulder in a soft glow, her abundant black hair flows down the back and slender arms held high. She is 'on show'. The camera closes in and she is revealed as a gorgeous young woman who looks simultaneously in pain and more than a bit pissed off with how things have gone down. The hooded brethren around Asa and the burly executioners – whose faces are obscured fully by hoods – are figures of male power and they look on unmoved.

PORTRAITS OF A LADY OCCULTIST

As mentioned, there are two portraits of Asa seen in the film. Both are unusual, but represent in visual form the tradition of women as either saints or whores. The first portrait we see hangs in the dining hall of the Vajda castle.

Asa stands in side profile. The background is given to a landscape of rolling hills. She wears a long gown, her arms are folded and the expression on the face, while typically demure, is uneasy. She looks like a bored aristocrat. The likeness to Steele is very apparent, too, and more so than the second painting.

Asa's portrait hangs in the Vajda castle living room

The other portrait of Asa is seen in the third act. It is a much rougher piece of work with Asa looking almost feral, and she is stark naked. She holds in her hands a crystal ball and an asp and is surrounded by great big leather-bound books and parchments. It is a very unusual portrait of a lady but also establishes her attitude to the conventions of social standing as well highlighting her demonic beliefs. The brazenness of this image is remarkable and it offers extra clues regarding Asa's life and religious practice.

The secret portrait discovered by Gorobec leads to the Vajda crypt

KATIA

If a fairy tale has a wicked witch then there must be a princess. The theme of demonic possession is strong in *Black Sunday*. It might have been ignored somewhat because everybody is still debating whether the villains are vampires or not. Asa wishes to take over the mind and body of Katia and to effectively transfer her soul and personality into the poor girl. Bava's decision to present Asa and Katia as visually indistinguishable – even their hairdos look the same – makes the theme of demonic possession richer, more irrational and nightmarish. Asa is already within Katia – her face is the face of Katia – and has informed her entire haunted life and understanding of the world. Taking over the body is the icing on the cake. Given the explicitly supernatural context of the plot, Katia's looks are not the result of a fine aristocratic lineage.

Constantine reminds his sister how the painting of Asa has been '*enthralled by that strange old painting*' since childhood. Katia replies: '*It holds danger for me … something alive about it; something mysterious about the eyes. That's it! They're vultures' eyes, somehow.*' Is it not particularly horrid to give this portrait such a prominent place in the Vajda house given its effect on poor Katia?

There is, too, another character in *Black Sunday* referred to as Princess Macha, who was 'mysteriously murdered', Prince Vajda claims, and is the same age as Katia. She, too, looked exactly like Asa. Prince Vajda quite rightly fears for his daughter's life. Katia is not the sweet and demure princess of tradition. She is essentially as tragic a figure as Asa, a woman living under the strict rule of a patriarchal society. She might well agree with Asa that it sucks being a lady of court in such a restrictive world. She is seen as a precious jewel by Prince Vajda, the father, and a potential love interest and wife material by Gorobec. Can't she be her own woman? *Black Sunday* cheated Katia of a scene in which she reflects on her life and fate. Gorobec notices Asa walking in the garden near the fountain. In *The Mask of Satan* we get a whole exchange between the pair which is absent from *Black Sunday* – as if the shot of Katia glumly staring into the fountain was enough when it really comes across as abrupt and unfocused. The scene starts with a panning shot from the trees to Asa standing by the fountain as Nicolosi's refrain – what can be called 'Katia's theme' – plays out. '*What is my life? It is sadness and grief; something that destroys itself day by day and no one can rebuild it,*' she tells Gorobec.

WHO IS JAVUTO?

Who is Javuto *exactly*? In AIP's version of the film, he is described by Griabe as Asa's '*serf*' before adding '*who you forced to do your bidding!*' We might well say he's a first-class doofus besotted with Asa and like Edward G. Robinson's Chris Cross in *Scarlet Street* (1945). Many a foolish man in the movies/history/literature was ruined by loving somebody unobtainable. (Asa is the archetypal *femme fatale*, don't forget.) She is therefore directly responsible for his death and we can feel pity for him. The dialogue is seemingly straightforward enough regarding the character, but something isn't quite right…

Javuto is dressed like a nobleman rather than some scuzzy peasant helper. The portrait in the Vajda castle, too, hangs pride of place next to the fireplace. His clothes bear a dragon emblem thus heavily suggesting he is a member of the Vajda family. Were the pair 'kissing cousins' or even more closely related? Is Javuto really Asa's brother and were the pair involved in a dangerous incestuous liaison that, once found out, along with all their interests in Satanism, vampires, whatever, condemned them to premature deaths at the hands of the Inquisition, conveniently led by their brother, Griabe? The original Italian credit for the character revealed just that: 'Prince Ygor Javutich – *fratello della stregia*', meaning, 'brother of the witch'. (In Croatia, vampires were known as '*pijavica*' and incest given as a cause of the transformation.) Given the secretive nature of their passion, is Javuto also responsible for that rather saucy, if unflattering, portrait of Asa?

WITCH OR VAMPIRE?

It has been noted since the film's release that *Black Sunday* appeared very much to confuse the terms 'witch' and 'vampire'. In fact, *Black Sunday* is entirely within the ever-changing and malleable vampire figure and the witch and keeps within the bounds of the concept laid out by Gogol's short story. The terms 'vampire' and 'witch' are linked throughout mythology and folklore: whether it's an etymological root or folkloric narratives that cross pollinated them. They are creatures bound by blood. The Russian form of the vampire - the 'eretica' – was a woman who had '*during life offered her soul to Satan in return for magical powers*' (Barlett & Idriceanu, 2005: 119). Alas, the 'eretica' is only active during spring and autumn, which puts the kibosh on Asa living for one hundred years on Katia's blood. *The Mask of Satan* does, however, take place on the Feast of St. George, placing that film's narrative right in the springtime.

Of course, none of this is an excuse for the plain inconsistencies present in *Black Sunday* in general. The narration during the opening sequence (AIP and *The Mask of Satan* cuts) mentions both witches and vampires, but the dialogue exchanges between Asa and Griabe do not make any reference to either vampires or vampirism. Only Voiceover Man puts the idea into our heads. Asa is convicted of being a vampire and yet she's clearly alive and doesn't appear to boast any of the mad skills Count Dracula has at his disposal (shape-shifting, etc.). The princess is to be given a witch's death, by immolation, after the

Mask of Satan has been hammered down onto her face. One can understand very well any confusion felt by the viewer. Yet, as Hall Baltimore (Val Kilmer) asked out loud in Francis Ford Coppola's *Twixt* (2011): *'What is a vampire but a witch that sucks blood?'*

Black Sunday begins with this introduction:

> One day in each century it is said that Satan walks amongst us. To the God-fearing, this day is known as 'Black Sunday'. In the 17th century the Devil appeared amidst the people of Moldavia. Those who served him were monstrous beings that thirsted for human blood. History has given these slaves of Satan the name 'vampire'. Whenever they were caught they were put to horrible deaths. Princess of Asa of the aristocratic Vajda family was one of these. She was sentenced to a witch's death by her own brother.

The Mask of Satan begins:

> In the 17th century, Satan was abroad on the Earth and great was the wrath against those monstrous beings, thirsty for human blood, to whom tradition has given the name 'vampires'. No appeal for pity or mercy was awarded. Family members did not hesitate to accuse brothers, and fathers accused sons, in the frantic attempt to purify the earth of that horrible race of blood thirsty devouring assassins.

When summing up her crimes, Griabe exclaims:

> Asa, daughter of the House of Vajda, this court of the Inquisition of Moldavia, has found you guilty. I, as the second born of the princes of Vajda – and as Grand Inquisitor – hereby condemn you. And as your brother, renounce you forever, severing the ties that bind us. This inquisition finds you not only guilty as a servant to Satan, but a high priestess to him!

The Mask of Satan runs:

> Asa, daughter of the House of Vajda, this high court of the Inquisition has declared you guilty. I, the second born son of Prince Vajda, as Grand Inquisitor, do condemn you. As your brother, I repudiate you. Too many evil deeds have you done to satisfy your monstrous love for that serf of the devil, Igor Javutich. May God have pity on your soul, in this your final hour.

It could be deemed highly strange and disappointing to set such a scene, explicitly suggesting vampires will be involved, and then refusing to give viewers the staples of the genre. And yet Bram Stoker's novel sees the evil Count packed off to hell without the traditional stake through the heart. He's stabbed by Quincey Morris' bowie knife and then beheaded. In *Black Sunday*, the crucifix is used as a tool in warding off evil. Prince Vajda's cross annoys Kruvajan during the scene in which he pretends to attend to the stricken old aristocrat. He informs Constantine and Katia to put the thing away on the pretext it might upset the old man: '*Take it away, it'll irritate him.*' Later on, Prince Vajda and Boris the servant bear the familiar fang marks which suggest the sucking of blood.

It is documented that Bava had his leading lady and her co-star wear plastic fangs (there's an extant production still of Dominici showing off the incisors) but changed his mind. There are two stories as to why he removed them. One is that Bava, ultimately, didn't like the way they appeared on camera and stated: '*I made the actors get rid of them because they were becoming a cliché even then*' (Lucas, 2007: 297). The other story version goes that Steele refused to wear them because they looked daft. Bava also claimed ignorance of vampire folklore and mythology:

> The strange thing is that I didn't know, before making this film, what vampires were. In our country, we have no vampires. As a child, I heard our maid tell us fables about Sardinian and Sicilian bandits, which terrified me, but I never heard of a vampire. In our country, the sun drives such things away. (ibid.)

It isn't quite right to claim as Matt Bailey does, in his essay on *Black Sunday* (Arrow Video booklet), that Bava created his own uncanny mythology. Betwixt wishing to avoid cliché and feigning ignorance, the film managed to align itself to the fog of folklore.

THE SATANIC LORD

Universal Pictures' success in 1931 with their adaptation of the stage play *Dracula* (adapted by Hamilton Deane then revised by John L. Balderston for the acclaimed Broadway run) and the movie sequels, proved immensely popular with audiences and continued the appreciation and fascination with the 'Satanic Lord' version of the vampire. Odell and Le Blanc noted that: 'The success and influence of Browning's Dracula is so immense that is can be difficult to view with real objectivity' (2008: 27).

In something of a key scene, Van Helsing (Edward Van Sloan) detailed the mythology widely adapted by subsequent movies. 'A vampire casts no reflection in the glass. That is why Dracula smashed the mirror.' Later, he tells Dr. Seward and a worried John Harker: 'A vampire, Mr. Harker, is a being that lives after its death by drinking the blood of the living. It must have blood or it dies. Its powers only last from sunset to sunrise. During the hours of the day it must rest in the earth in which it was buried.'

Count Dracula and other vampire figures, as with the most popular literary incarnation, found popularity as sleek and seductive individuals that slept in coffins in dank crypts, and mesmerised victims, often young ladies. That Black Sunday dispensed or altered these elements somewhat doesn't make it problematic or the film inauthentic. Bava managed to dig into a mélange of 17th century cases of vampirism and the Romantic/Gothic figure that arose from John Polidori's short story, The Vampyre (1819). Here we have what Leonard Wolf called (cited in Legends of Blood, 2005) the 'prototype vampire' who was a 'nobleman, aloof, brilliant, chilling, fascinating to women, and coolly evil' (2005: 32).

The doomed physician/author modeled his Lord Ruthven character on Lord Byron, a former patient and man long suspected of a Javuto-like affection for his sister. In the 1920s Montague Summers (1880–1948), an author and man of the cloth who believed unequivocally in the world of the supernatural, authored two books titled Vampires, His Kith and Kin (1928) and The Vampire in Europe (1929). Summers noted (cited in Legend of Blood): 'throughout the shadowy world of ghosts and demons there is no figure so terrible, no figure so dreaded and abhorred, yet dight with such fascination, as the vampire, who is himself neither ghost or demon, but who partakes the dark natures and possesses the mysterious and terrible qualities of both' (2005: 7).

As we can deduce from that quote, far from clearing up the matter at hand, he 'succeeded in only in showing how difficult it is to define the characteristics that exclusively belonged to the vampire,' according to Christopher Frayling (1991: 5). We might well take the voiceover narration of Black Sunday as getting its genres confused, but some reports written in the wake of the notorious Arnold Paole case concluded that what was happening was 'the work of Satan' and 'the vampire was Satan' (ibid: 45).

A Romanian variation of the vampire is the Strigoi, a word whose origin has been disputed. The etymological root of the word is said to be from the old Italian for 'witchcraft' – *stregheria*. Psychoanalyst Ernest Jones' *On the Nightmare* (1931), explored vampirism from a Freudian perspective and the notion of 'haemosexuality':

> The word 'Vampire' itself, introduced into general European use towards the end of the first third of the eighteenth century, is a Southern Slav word. Its derivation has been much disputed, but the great authority, Miklosch, considers the most likely one to be the North Turkish *uber*, a witch. (ibid: 414)

The first cinematic vampires were not the kind we now associate with the term at all. 'Vamps' were proto *femme fatales* and would later resurface in film noir and gangster pictures. Early screen incarnations included Musidora as Irma Vep (an anagram of 'vampire') in Louis Feuillade's serial, *Les Vampires* (1915), or Hollywood superstar, Theda Bara (a name the PR team announced was an anagram of Arab Death, for extra exotic allure).

> In essence, there are four archetypal vampires in nineteenth-century fiction: the Satanic Lord (Polidori and others), the Fatal Woman (Tieck, Hoffmann, Gautier, Baudelaire, Swinburne and Le Fanu), the Unseen Force (O'Brien and de Maupassant) and the Folkloric Vampire (Merimee, Gogol, Tolstoy, Turgenev, Linton and Burton). (ibid: 62)

The movies jumped on the Satanic Lord and Fatal Woman variations proving that sex plays a huge part in their appeal, whether that's Count Dracula, a babe from a Jean Rollin skin flick or Edward Cullen from *The Twilight Saga*. *Black Sunday* presented a heady mixture of three vampire types found in 19th century literature: the Folkloric, the Fatal Woman and the Satanic Lord.

The Folkloric aspect of *Black Sunday* occurred via the Moldavian setting, use of Nikolai Gogol's source material, the time period between 1630-1830, and the unusual methods in which Asa, Javuto, Kruvajan and Prince Vajda are killed off in the third act. *Black Sunday* does not concern itself too much with commoners (or their superstitions) bar the ending and peripheral figures such as the Innkeeper, her daughter or the drunken coach driver. The narrative is set within a decayed aristocratic milieu far removed from the sophisticated worlds of Paris and London. Voltaire found the whole idea of vampires laughable and pointed out in a supplement to his *Dictionaire Philosophique*: '*What! Vampires in our Eighteenth Century? Yes … in Poland, Hungary, Silesia, Moravia, Austria and Lorraine – there is no talk of vampires in London, or even Paris*' (1991: 30).

'*Our ways are not your ways,*' Count Dracula tells Jonathan Harker. Eastern Europe was the spiritual-political battle ground between Catholicism and the Orthodox Church: the place still part of Europe and yet outside the sphere of overt western influence. Mystery and exoticism arose along with a sense of the unknowable and wild things. 'Transylvania' translates in Romanian to 'the land beyond the forest'. It's the perfect place for monsters to thrive.

Although the aristocratic vampire incarnation fed off the plebs – literally – he doesn't have a particular rapport with them or see them as anything other than victims in life *or* death, or hired help. The Archbishop of Trani, Giuseppe Davanzanti commented during the vampire scare/craze: '*Why is this demon so partial to base-born plebians?*' (ibid: 30). Exactly because it reflected a culture and tradition in which aristocrats – alive or undead – believed they were above the law and could act with impunity! It's the Marxist class system become Darwinian food chain.

Black Sunday fits in neatly enough to the folkloric vampire figure – from accounts written in the 17th and 18th century – as they were known to return to the family and attack their relatives. In the cases of Guire Grando and Peter Plogojowitz, both were said to have attacked their relatives and acquaintances.

Learned men of Europe – in a post-Enlightenment age – were baffled by the fad for vampires and horror stories coming out of the darkest corners of the continent. More than a few philosophers, religious clerics and scientifically-minded writers suspected local priests to be drumming up fear as part of a power play. The actions of Asa and Javuto are not the same as Count Dracula (novel) or Hammer's version of the character. Theirs is exclusively a plot involving resurrection, secrecy and vengeance. It is never stated what Asa's aims are beyond killing her ancestors even though Javuto states, '*Through her blood your destiny will be fulfilled*' and '*For the next hundred years her blood will keep you living.*' Perhaps the height of Asa's plot is to keep on keeping on in the evil department and be immortal once again… rather modest enough aims for the undead, no?

6. BLACK SUNDAY'S LEGACY

Black Sunday would be paid deference and homage throughout the 1960s and beyond. Its influence is frankly massive. Film-makers fell over themselves in casting Barbara Steele and she became a Scream Queen (reluctant or not). Roger Corman hired Steele for *The Pit and the Pendulum* (1961) and ended the film with Steele's face encased in metal. Elsewhere, directors found it entirely within their remit to riff on the opening scene and so it entered film history as one of the most iconic in horror cinema. Films such as *The Torture Chamber of Dr. Sadism* (1967), starring Christopher Lee as the wicked Count Regula, incorporated the use of a mask as a torture device (in its opening scene, too). Even posters sought to reference *Black Sunday*. One promo, that advertised Mexico's *The Curse of the Crying Woman* (1963), recreated (in essence) the shot of Katia holding her Great Danes.

Michael Reeves, whose life was tragically cut short by a drug overdose in 1969, was inspired by Bava. In *Revenge of the Blood Beast* (1965), another flick about a revived witch, the young director cast Barbara Steele. But was his opening to the bleak and despairing Tigon picture, *Witchfinder General* (1968), a creative response to *Black Sunday*, divested of the monochromatic sheen and the glamour and beauty of its leading lady?

Witchfinder General begins with an elderly crone, having been found guilty of witchcraft, dragged up onto a Suffolk hillside and hanged before a crowd of onlookers. Stylistically, the two sequences are poles apart. One is the product of Gothic imagination and the other a grim historical recreation. Both feature repellent violence against women and both start their films with memorable displays of power and sadism against female characters.

Black Sunday's influence was not only felt in the movies. Marvel man Jack Kirby, according to Tim Lucas, used the central Mask of Satan image and the character Javuto as inspiration for Doctor Doom (along with his backstory involving being the son of an Eastern European witch). Lucas also posited the idea that since Doctor Doom was an influence on Darth Vader in *Star Wars* (1977), we can trace it all back to Bava's film and its release in the United States.

In later years, the influence could still be gleaned in such films as Tobe Hooper's *Lifeforce* (1985), which featured a gorgeous and completely naked female vampire (known only as Space Girl) awoken from her slumber. She drains victims in exactly the same manner as Asa – by kiss and/or touch alone – though Hooper had an outrageously grand budget, shot on70mm and could do all sorts of wonderful electronic effects whereas Bava did it with coloured gauzes and a dab of grease paint.

Tim Burton has made several forays into the horror genre. In *Sleepy Hollow* (1999), a dream sequence recounts the time Icabod Crane's mother was encased in an Iron Maiden torture device. The mother (played Lisa Marie) suffered facial puncture wounds highly reminiscent of Princess Asa's. In 2012's *Dark Shadows*, Burton once again referenced Bava's debut. Elizabeth Collins Stoddard (Michelle Pfieffer) and her vampire ancestor, Barnabas Collins, played by Johnny Depp, walk through a secret passageway accessed via a fireplace (as in *Black Sunday*). Noticing that Barnabas does not cast a reflection in the mirror, the lantern held by the vampire hangs in empty space, just as when Kruvajan notices, with some terror, the suspended lantern previously held by Javuto. Later on, Bella Heathcote, in dual roles as Victoria Winters and Josette DuPres (another homage/link), walks towards a cliff-top. Burton, effectively, restages Sonya's trip to the cow shed. It is worth pointing out, too, that the director offered Barbara Steele a cameo appearance in *Dark Shadows*, but she demurred.

Burton commented on the film's impact: '*Black Sunday is one of those movies – and this happens to you mainly as a child – that leaves an impression on you, and you don't necessarily know why*' (Salisbury 2006: 173).

Even today, Bava and Bavian imagery can be detected in a range of movies and television shows. In Joss Whedon's *Buffy the Vampire Slayer* (1997–2003), Buffy, lying rotting in her grave, in the opening episodes of season 6, is dressed in black like Asa, complete with empty eye sockets. Rob Zombie's *The Lords of Salem* (2012) also doffs its cap to *Black Sunday*. Critics duly noted in Ryan Gosling's *Lost River*, which premiered at Festival de Cannes in 2014, the influence of Mario Bava. Barbara Steele makes a cameo appearance, furthering Gosling's desire to pay homage.

Tim Burton's homage to Princess Asa and Black Sunday

MARIO BAVA'S DRACULA

Francis Ford Coppola's 1992 feature, *Bram Stoker's Dracula*, could be retitled 'Mario Bava's Dracula'. The film works perfectly well as a standard Hollywood blockbuster by a celebrated director. But if you're familiar with the Italian's filmography the American adaptation feels deeply indebted to the kind of technical ingenuity, poetic beats and sudden explosive violence showcased in Bava's first picture, and throughout his whole career.

'*I decided I was going to make Dracula like a movie magician working in London 1897,*' Francis told *Starbust* magazine (no.175, 1993). The extensive use of glass matte paintings and in-camera trick photography might not be exclusively Bava, but it is pure Bava in spirit and far more sophisticated than a film-maker working in London circa 1897 could ever have marshalled on celluloid. As far back as 1977 writer David Pirie lamented in his book, *The Vampire Cinema*, that he found it '*more regrettable than ever that Bava never worked on a Dracula movie*' (1977: 161).

One does not wish to over-egg the pudding, but as a Mario Bava geek, viewing *Bram Stoker's Dracula* is akin to a revelation. His hand feels all over it and the movie reads like a gorgeously penned love letter to *Black Sunday*. Fans might well imagine if this is what the Italian's *Dracula* would have been like had he produced an adaptation himself. You only have to watch Harker's arrival in Transylvania to see the influence all over it like a klieg light. Coppola, talking to the press, name-checked big boys such as Jean Cocteau (also an influence on Bava) and F.W. Murnau (the 1992 film does share the same melancholy spirit as *Nosferatu*) as his artistic luminaries, but the sensibility of Coppola is Italian to a T.'*My father taught us to steal from the best!*' Coppola declared to Cinefantastique (April 1993). Bava *was* the best.

A gloomy forest with overhanging branches in Bram Stoker's Dracula (1992) could be an image from Black Sunday

Roman Coppola worked on his dad's picture as an assistant director and oversaw much of the 2nd unit. The Coppolas hired Matte World to devise the special effects after initially approaching CG designers to help recreate Victorian Britain and Transylvania. *Dracula*'s cavalcade of ingenious photography and in-camera ricks is utterly indebted to *Black Sunday* because it's so complete and encompassing as part of the conceptual framework. One sequence does reference the movie explicitly: Jonathan Harker's journey to the Borgo Pass, his brief wait by the side of the country road and the arrival of the black carriage approaching in slow motion. The scene is a recreation of Javuto's beautifully eerie phantom carriage ride through the countryside on his way to pick up Kruvajan as witnessed by the Innkeeper's daughter. Before that we get misty landscapes and branches like spindly fingers framing shots. One can almost imagine Harker bumping into a loitering Kruvajan, as the elderly physician smokes his pipe by the little pond. Roman Coppola was interviewed for the documentary *Operazione Paura*:

I first seemed to be aware of his [Bava] work when I was preparing for *Dracula*, my dad's version of *Dracula*. In *Black Sunday*, there's a scene where they're riding in a carriage and it's clear that the tree branches are just going by without the carriage actually moving and that's something we did in *Dracula*. We borrowed that technique. That's an old movie trick, but it's done in a very wonderful way. (2004)

A direct reference to Black Sunday as the phantom carriage approaches Jonathan Harker.

Coppola Jr. would later go on to direct *CQ* (2000), a movie about the clash between art and commerce in the world of film-making that paid direct tribute to Bava's spy thriller *Diabolik* (1968). Michael Pangrazio, director of effects photography and miniatures on *Dracula*, related to *Cinefantastique* (Vol 23, Issue 6) how he and the crew designed shots of the night sky as Harker arrives at Castle Dracula. Bava would no doubt have enjoyed the old-school approach and practical cinema magic.

We had a sheet of glass with some vaseline on it, between the model and the camera, to flare out the moonlight. The moving clouds were suspended on horizontal wires attached to a motorized track. (1993: 55)

But can we push the *Mario Bava's Dracula* notion further still? One of the main bones of contention with the 1992 film is the performance of Keanu Reeves as Jonathan

Harker. It often polls in Worst Performance listicles, including *Total Film*'s Most Wooden Performances (August 2009). It feels like critics have missed something in their rush to lay the blame and projected all their dislike about aspects of the picture on to poor Mr. Reeves. The film delivered an emotional intensity Stoker himself might have found embarrassingly overwrought. (It has been suggested he didn't quite understand the erotic charge of his own novel.) The plummy delivery of what is at times the totally crummy cod-poetic dialogue heard in *Black Sunday* spoken by the actors in a sort of overstated manner recalls the dubbing work made by AIP. Coppola's decision to render his story in an old-fashioned style is entirely part of the concept and not simply actors being allowed to get away with dodgy performances. Think about it. Why on God's green earth would a director of such fastidiousness and creativity as Francis Ford Coppola – one of modern American cinema's most incredible and maverick talents – suddenly allow 'accents' to ruin his opus? Everything is there for a reason. Winona Ryder, Sadie Frost, Gary Oldman and Anthony Hopkins all bring on the *jambon*. It tastes delicious.

La maschera del demonio remade

Movies have always been remade by other hands (sometimes directors even revisit their own past hits and update them – even Bava was tempted to do so). Remakes are not the sole preserve of lazy modern studios, despite common prejudice. Remakes happen because: A) the original made a lot of money first time round and therefore in theory can again; B) they have become iconic movies deeply embedded in popular culture; C) that very audience recognition means a great amount of interest and marketability.

Fans do like to vent and moan on online forums, but on release day they – like supreme masochists – go and pay their good money for a ticket to squirm in their seats at the latest 'desecration' of their favourite horror film. *La maschera del demonio* was remade not by some Hollywood hack or studio but Mario's boy, Lamberto. However, it's not strictly a remake and more a case of incorporating key imagery and ideas. Neither was it marketed in foreign territories as '*Black Sunday*' (not even in America, where it received a home video release).

Like his father, Lamberto has worked mostly within the genre confines of fantasy and horror. He is a respected figure and, at times, has demonstrated that he can be a film-maker with skill and purpose. In the 1980s, he collaborated with Dario Argento on several celebrated pictures.

Lamberto Bava made his directorial debut with *Macabre* (1980) having spent years working with dear old dad, including co-authoring the script for *Shock* (1977). After plum gigs as an assistant director to Argento on *Inferno* (1980) and *Tenebrae* (1983), Lamberto returned to the director's chair with *Blade in the Dark* (1983). 1985's *Demons*, however, is the movie that cemented his own name and reputation with horror fans across the world.

The *Demons* series, made when Italian genre cinema was at death's door, mixed together a music video aesthetic, heavy metal soundtracks and exquisitely gooey special effects work by Sergio Stivaletti. *Demons* feeds on a garish and ludicrous tone and the first two pictures in the series have become confirmed cult classics thanks to their winning combo of nightmarish narrative, violent sensations and the utter abandonment of logic. Therein lays its charm. The comic message appeared to be: yes, the movies can have effect on the viewer by turning them – literally – into psychopathic creatures (a censorship board's worst case scenario).

Demons takes place in a Berlin movie theatre with specially invited patrons succumbing to a virus transmitted by the big screen that sees them mutate into bestial monsters that wallow in their own slime and debasement. The series spawned a direct sequel, also directed by Lamberto Bava, and three unofficial sequels, one of which aligned itself to Mario Bava's debut.

A European co-production, *La mascheria del demonio* (1989) was sold in America (on VHS) as *Demons 5: The Devil's Veil* rather than reusing the AIP title (even if today English-speaking fans refer to it as 'the *Black Sunday* remake'). The film suffered from very limited distribution. Lamberto's take on the material is in no danger of clouding over the original *La maschera del demonio*, nor *The Mask of Satan* or *Black Sunday* any time soon. There is zero chance of it being labelled as anything than a curiosity object for cult movie aficionados and very possibly of academic interest alone. The most likely audience response to the 1989 *La maschera del demonio* is laughter. Yes, it is cheesier than a quattro fromaggio pizza, thanks to the outrageous 1980s gloss, the dated costume design, bouffant hairdos and aesthetic that screams more Adrian Lyne than Mario Bava. It is enjoyable enough in its own way – just don't expect anything special.

The screenplay was by Massimo De Rita and Giorgio Stegani and depicts a group of young skiers uncovering the ancient resting place of the dead witch, Anibas, after a crevasse opens in the ice and they fall down into it. The frozen corpse in the ice wears a mask (which is utterly unremarkable and bears more of a resemblance to *Friday the 13th* slasher icon Jason Vorhees than Eugenio Bava's refined artistry). The group, led by David and Sabina (take a good look at that latter name), come unstuck when slowly the spirit of the witch wreaks havoc on the group turning them into sex-obsessed demons and attempts to take control of Sabina's body in order to provide her own resurrection.

The film is Gothic cinema wedded to the gloss of advertising and music videos. As mentioned, the cinematography by Gianfranco Transunto and vibe of the film is as far from Gothic elegance as can be imagined. If Mario Bava photographed Barbara Steele in the manner of a fetish object then Lamberto seems more inspired by porno mags and softcore videos. Eva Grimaldi (Anibas) and Debora Caprioglio (Sabina) are unavoidably lost in Asa/Steele's mighty shadow no matter how beautiful in their own right. There is a giant difference between eroticism and cheap titillation. But Lamberto setting up his own film and path is to be applauded.

The keen viewer or avid fan will be amused by the few references made to the father's movie, including a direct homage to the claustrophobic shot in which the audience – for the briefest of moments – peers through the Mask of Satan as it approaches the terrified face of Anibas. The film also replicated the opening torture sequence, though this time it occurs half an hour in, and as a flashback. Anibas's face is studded with spiked marks and the curse motif is reused but with less convincing effect. *Demons 5/La machera del demonio*, essentially, is a post modernist stew of Mario's debut, the *Demons* series and the production of *Viy*, made in 1967, by Mosfilm in Russia.

Lamberto Bava, interviewed by *Fluster* magazine, commented on the film:

> It is a movie I'd love to watch again, but I've never managed to find a copy of it. I
> remember it as a movie with great special effects by Stivaletti, the plot wasn't bad,

maybe the actors weren't the best, but it was very different from my father's under the stylistic aspect. (2011)

AFTER BLACK SUNDAY

Mario Bava returned to the Gothic throughout his career. As well the 'Vourdelak' segment in *Black Sabbath*, he made *The Whip and the Body*, starring Christopher Lee and Daliah Lavi, and his later masterpiece, *Kill, Baby … Kill!* in 1966. Even if *Baron Blood* (1972) and *Lisa and the Devil* (1973) incorporated Gothic horror tropes, '*Kill, Baby … Kill!* brought the curtain down on the golden age of Italian fantasy that had begun with I vampiri' (Lucas, 2013: 57).

Bava earned a name for himself by helping to establish *gialli* thrillers in Italy. *The Telephone* short in *Black Sabbath*, *The Girl Who Knew Too Much* (1963) and *Blood and Black Lace* (1964) helped kick-start the trend. His sole outing in sci-fi horror, *Planet of the Vampires* (1965), would be a huge stylistic influence on Ridley Scott's *Alien* (whether anybody working on the 1979 classic wanted to admit it or not) and the proto-slasher, *Reazione a catena* (*A Bay of Blood* and also known as *Twitch of the Death Nerve*, 1971), was a vital inspiration on *Friday The 13th* (1980) and others that followed in its bloody wake. *Rabid Dogs* (1974) has been discussed in recent years as one of many influences on Quentin Tarantino's *Reservoir Dogs* (1991). Quite possibly (along with Roger Corman) Mario Bava is the most influential genre filmmaker the medium has ever known. His career, however, ended more with a whimper than a bang. Distribution issues and other problems arose. *Lisa and the Devil*, a classy chiller, was turned into a blatant rip-off of *The Exorcist* (1973) after producer Alfredo Leone decided the film needed to be more like William Friedkin's shocker. It was retitled *House of Exorcism* with an entirely new scenario and scenes grafted onto footage shot by Bava. The exorcism scenes are beyond bad and the foul-mouthed, blasphemous dialogue is absolute trash. The director attempted to placate Leone and his re-worked vision – after all, he improvised a lot on set himself – but eventually, dejected by the experience, he disowned it. Today, fans can see the original – and infinitely classier – cut of *Lisa and the Devil*, thanks to the recent release by Arrow Video (and others).

Suffering a fatal heart attack as he slept, Bava died on 25th April, 1980. He was sixty-five years old.

CONCLUSION

The traditional Gothic ambience, the surrealist-tinged irrationality, the fairy tale plot and graphic violence combined to make *Black Sunday* stand out from the crowd and the film has remained highly regarded over half a century on. In *Time Out*'s 2012 survey of '100 Best Horror Films', *Black Sunday* was ranked 84th. The list was derived from a variety of critics, directors and industry experts, including this author.

In 1998 as part of a National Film Theatre retrospective of Bava's career in the movies titled *Blood and Black Celluloid*, Alan Jones commented in the NFT programme guide how the director's filmography was '*often atrociously dubbed, appallingly retitled, re-edited by distributors, cut by censors, and dumped in the bottom half of exploitation double bills*' (Jones, 1998: 16).

The Italian maestro of the macabre – Signor Horror – did indeed suffer the slings and arrows of other people's often barbarous actions. But so well-crafted were these pictures, no matter how hampered by the decisions of others, something shone through regardless. That is a true testament to Bava's talent and the ability to capture the attention of the critics and movie fans worldwide. Very few films can be put together in such an experimental, even clumsy, fashion, be so full of plot holes that make it the equivalent of Swiss cheese, exist in multiple versions (with as many titles) and reworked to sate the demands of distributors and censors around the world, and yet – and yet – still boast enduring appeal and fascination. It's frankly remarkable.

Chiaroscuro lighting; compositions that defied the spatial limitations of the soundstage when not revelling in their artificiality; the painterly framing; the grotty violence; the velvety camera movements; the whip pans and crash zooms, the inventiveness of the miniatures and other special effects (a movie shot not only on what we'd call today a shoestring budget but possibly featuring actual shoestrings) and Steele's mesmerising face in close-up: all combined to make *Black Sunday* a *tour de force* that punched well above its weight. We are turned on not only by Steele's black widow allure as Asa and captivated by the sullenness of Katia, but also the sheer orgasmic joy of the poetic imagery presented by Bava. *Black Sunday*: the quintessence of fatal beauty and cinema's beguiling dream reality.

BIBLIOGRAPHY

Abbot, S. (2002) 'The Vampire Transformed', in *Kinoeye*, Vol 2, Issue 18 http://www.kinoeye.org/02/18/abbott18.php

Adair, G. (1995) *Flickers: An Illustrated History of 100 Years of Cinema*. London: Faber & Faber

Barlett, W. & Idriceanu, F. (2005) *Legends of Blood: The Vampire in History and Mythology*. Stroud: Sutton Publishing

Baschiera, S. & Di Chiara, F. (2010) 'Once Upon A Time in Italy: Transnational Features of Genre Production 1960s-1970s', in *Film Int*. Vol. 8. No.6

Bataille, G. (Dalwood, M., trans.) (1986) *Eroticism: Death and Sensuality*. New York: City Lights Books

Bayman, L. (2011) *Directory of World Cinema: Italy*. Bristol: Intellect Publishing

Bava, L. (2011) *Fluster* magazine http://flustermagazine.com/2011/11/09/interview-with-lamberto-bava/

Bell, J. (ed.) (2013) *BFI Gothic Compendium*. London: BFI

Butler, I. (1979) *Horror in the Cinema*. New Jersey: A.S. Barnes and Co, Inc.

Burton, T. (2004) *Operazione Paura*. Italy: Sky Cinema (dir: Acerbo, G. & Pisoni, R.)

Caputo, R. (1997) 'Blood and Black Celluloid' in *Metro* magazine (Issue 110, 1997)

Clarens, C. (1968) *Horror Movies, An Illustrated Survey*. New York: Paragon

Coppola, R. (2004) *Operazione Paura*. Italy: Sky Cinema (dir: Acerbo, G. & Pisoni, R.)

Corman, R. (2004) *Operazione Paura*. Italy: Sky Cinema (dir: Acerbo, G. & Pisoni, R.)

Cook, P. (2007) *The Cinema Book* (3rd edition). London: BFI

Derry, C. (2009) *Dark Dreams 2.0*. USA: McFarland & Co

Forshaw, B. in Bell, J. (ed.) (2013) *BFI Gothic Compendium*. London: BFI

Frayling, C. (1981) *Spaghetti Westerns: Cowboys and Europeans from Karl May to Sergio Leone*. London: I.B. Tauris

Frayling, C. (1991) *Vampyres: Lord Byron to Dracula*. London: Faber and Faber

Petley, J. (1982) 'City of the Living Dead review', in *Films and Filming*. London

Goodwen, D. http://www.totalfilm.com/features/the-most-wooden-movie-performances (6 September 2013)

Greene, G. (1935, 1980) in Taylor, J. (ed.) *The Pleasure Dome: The Collected Film Criticism (1935–40)*. Oxford: Oxford University Press

Gogol, N. (Pevear, R. & Volokhonsky, L., trans.) (2008) *The Collected Tales*. London: Everyman Library

Hoyveda, F. (1961) quoted in Caputo, R. (1997) 'Blood and Black Celluloid' in *Metro* magazine (Issue 110, 1997)

Hughes, H. (2011) *Cinema Italiano*. London: I.B. Tauris

Janisse, Kier-La (2012) *House of Psychotic Women*. Godalming: FAB Press

Jones, A. (2013) *Black Sunday* Arrow Video Booklet

Jones, A. (1998) NFT Programme (August). London: BFI

Kermode, M. (2013) *Hatchet Job*. London: Picador

Landis, J. (2004) *Operazione Paura*. Italy: Sky Cinema (dir: Acerbo, G. & Pisoni, R.)

Lovecraft, H.P. (1982) *The Best of Lovecraft*. New York: Ballantine Books

Lucas, T. (1997) 'Reinventing The Mask of Satan', *Metro* magazine, Issue 110, 1997

Lucas, T. (2007) *Mario Bava: All The Colours of the Dark*. Ohio: Video Watchdog

Lucas, T. (2013) Audio commentary track on *Black Sunday*, Region 2, Arrow Video release

Milne, T. (1968) *Film Monthly Bulletin*, August

McNab, G. (2012), *The Guardian* 'Barbara Steele' Interview, London http://www.guardian.co.uk/film/2011/jul/21/barbara-steele-roger-corman

Mete, P. in Schneider, S. J. (ed.) (2009) *101 Horror Movies You Must See Before You Die.* New York: Cassell Illustrated

Newman, K. (1988) *Nightmare Movies* (revised edition). London: Bloomsbury

Nowell-Smith G., Hay, J. & Volpi, G. (1996) *The Companion to Italian Cinema.* London: BFI/Cassell

Nugent, C. (1983) *Masks of Satan.* London: Sheed & Ward

Odell, C. & Le Blanc, M. (2008) *Vampire Films.* Harpenden: Pocket Essentials

Pirie, D. (1977) *The Vampire Cinema.* London: Hamlyn

Praz, M. (1933) *The Romantic Agony.* Oxford: Oxford University Press

Rattigan, D. (2012) Barbara Steele Interview, *Diabolique* website http://diaboliquemagazine.com/interview-barbara-steele/

Roud, R. (1980) *Cinema: A Critical Dictionary, Vol. 1 A– K.* London: Secker and Warburg

Roszak, T. (1992) *Flicker.* London: Bantam New Fiction

Salisbury, M. (2006) *Burton on Burton.* London: Faber & Faber

Sarris, A. (1962) 'Notes on the Auteur Theory' in *Film Culture*, 1962

Schneider, S. J. (ed.) (2009) *101 Horror Movies You Must See Before You Die.* New York: Cassell Illustrated

Shelley, P. (1895) *The Poetical Works: Percy Bysshe Shelley.* London: George Routledge & Sons

Steele, B. (1983) *Halls of Horror*, vol 2. Issue 26. Reprinted by *Diabolique* magazine (2010) http://diaboliquemagazine.com/interview-barbara-steele/

Steele, B. (2013) Interview on the Arrow Video release of *Black Sunday* Blu-ray Extra Features

Stoker, B. (1897) *Dracula*, London: Wordsworth Classics

Tombs, P. & Tohill, C. (1994) *Immoral Tales: Sex and Horror Cinema in Europe 1956–1984*. London: Primitive Press

Torok, J.P. (1961) quoted in Caputo, R. (1997) 'Blood and Black Celluloid' in *Metro* magazine (Issue 110, 1997)

Tolstoy, A. (1884) *The Family of the Vourdalak* cited in Frayling, C. (1991) *Vampyres: Lord Byron to Dracula*. London: Faber and Faber

Trevelyan, J. (1973) *What The Censor Saw*. London: Michael Joseph

Wolf, L. (1993, 1897) *Dracula* – 'Introduction'. Pan Books: London

DEVIL'S ADVOCATES

"Auteur Publishing's new Devil's Advocates critiques on individual titles offer bracingly fresh perspectives from passionate writers. The series will perfectly complement the BFI archive volumes." Christopher Fowler, Independent on Sunday

THE THING — JEZ CONOLLY

"A fascinating, detailed analysis of Carpenter's framing and character positioning... will change the way you view the movie, as will much of Conolly's writing... comes with the kind of wit and enthusiasm that put other, more po-faced analyses of horror movies to shame." – Frightfest.co.uk

THE DESCENT — JAMES MARRIOTT

"James Marriott makes a strong case for [The Descent] being the finest example of the films that revitalised the genre in the early years of the new millennium... This is probably the best Devil's Advocate volume that I've yet seen, an absorbing account of a film that could so easily be dismissed as just an action come horror outing..." – Black Static

CARRIE — NEIL MITCHELL

"Top-notch... accessible, insightful." – Total Film

"...[goes] into exhaustive detail on the genesis of the film... a brisk, enjoyable read [5 stars]." – Frightfest.co.uk

HALLOWEEN — MURRAY LEEDER

"Murray Leeder's thoughtful, clearly expressed analysis of Halloween is far reaching in scope while resisting the temptation to become sidetracked... Leeder's book is a joy to read; it's insightful and well researched and serves as an encouragement to return to Halloween once again..." – Exquisite Terror

Printed and bound by CPI Group (UK) Ltd, Croydon, CR0 4YY

13/04/2025

14656601-0002